itchy BUSINESS

*How to Treat the Poison Ivy and Poison Oak Rash,
Prevent Exposure and Eradicate the Plant*

by

Amy Martin

*to Natasha~
Who inspires me
Amy Martin*

www.Itchy.Biz

©2016 Amy Martin

All rights reserved. The written consent of Amy Martin is required
to reproduce any part of this book, including by photocopy
or electronic text.

First printing March 2016

Printed in the United States of America

TABLE OF CONTENTS

Section 1:
The Big Itchy Picture

Chapter 1:
Poison Oak and Poison Ivy: Weirder Than You Know ~ 5
- The Rash and You
- The Stages of PI Rash
- When it Comes to PI, it's Personal

Section 2:
Understanding Urushiol

Chapter 1:
Urushiol, Your Foe ~ 10
- Urushiol: Understand the Allergen to Outwit It
- Who's Allergic, Who's Not, and How That Changes
- Levels of Misery: Why Some Rashes Are Worse Than Others
- No Such Luck: De-sensitizing the Body to Urushiol

Chapter 2:
Cleaning Off Urushiol ~ 13
- Within 5 minutes: Water
- Within an Hour: Detergent, Alcohol and Oxygen
- Within a Day: Solvents
- If the Rash Appears: Scrubs
- In the Field: What Not to Do
- Post-Cleaning Skin Care

Section 3:
Rash Mastery

Chapter 1:
Rash 101 ~ 18
- The Skin: First Line of Defense
- Mob Mentality: How Allergic Overreaction Creates the Rash

Chapter 2:
It's All About That Itch ~ 21
- What Is Itch?
- Be a PI Ninja
- Transcend the Itch
- Holistic: For the Long Run

Chapter 3:
When the Rash Goes Bad ~ 24
- When to See a Doctor - Fast!
- What a Doctor Can Do
- Steroids: Relief at a Price
- Speaking Derma-Doc Talk
- The Hell of Inhalation

Section 4:
Your Rash Toolkit

Chapter 1:
Practice Safe Scratch ~ 28
- Soft Friction
- Extreme Heat
- Extreme Cold
- Acids and Alkalines
- Counter-irritants
- Food Enzymes
- Night Gloves

Chapter 2:
The Stages:
Your Key To Rash Relief ~ 32
- Stage 1: Interrupt the Rash
- Stage 2: Master the Itch
- Stage 2: Manage the Blisters
- Stage 3: Heal the Skin

Chapter 3:
The Cs of Itch Relief ~ 34
- Calm: Soothers
- Cool: Aromatics
- Constrict: Astringents

Chapter4:
Plants and Minerals for Rash ~ 35
- Glossary: From A to Z
- From Potions to Lotions: How to Apply Them

Section 5:
Rash Remedies

Chapter 1:
Stage 1 - Interrupting the Rash ~ 45
- Topical Steroids
- Topical Herbs
- Oxygen Creams
- Homeopathics
- Oral Antihistamines

Chapter 2:
Stage 2 - Calming the Rash ~ 48
- Topical Earth
- Topical Herbs
- Water-Based Relief
- Kitchen Alkalines

Chapter 3:
Stage 2 - Cooling the Itch ~ 55
- Topical Earth
- Topical Herbs
- Water-Based Relief
- Kitchen Remedies

Chapter 4:
Stage 3 - Constricting the Blisters ~ 59
- Topical Earth
- Witch Hazel
- Other Astringents
- Salicylic Acid
- Topical Herbs
- Water-Based Relief

Chapter5:
Stages 2 and 3 - Analgesics for Pain Relief ~ 64
- Sprays
- Creams and Lotions

Chapter 6:
Stage 4 - Repairing the Skin ~ 66
- How to Repair Your Skin
- Topical Herbs
- Water-Based Relief

Chapter 7:
Holistic: Treat the Body, Reduce the Rash ~ 71
- Vitamins and Supplements
- Make Your Gut Happy
- Alkalize Your Body
- Low Histamine Diet
- Acupuncture
- Ayurvedic
- Homeopathy

Section 6:
Identifying the Plant

Chapter 1:
The American Axis of Itching ~ 76
- Four Main Species and Where They Grow
- Poison Sumac: the Swamp Monster

Chapter 2:
Know Your Adversary ~ 81
- PI Identification Basics
- Identifying PI In All Places & Seasons
- Innocent Imitators

Section 7:
Defending Yourself

Chapter 1:
Prevent Skin Contact ~ 88
- Barrier Lotions
- Protective Clothing
- Dealing with Nuclear Clothes
- Better Habits

Chapter 2:
Prevent Secondary Exposure ~ 92
- Weird & Tragic Ways We Spread Urushiol Around
- How To Clean Everything

Section 8:
Eradicating the Plant

Chapter 1:
Prepare for Battle ~ 97
- Combat Gear
- Timing: When To Wage Battle

Chapter 2:
Bye, Bye, PI ~ 100
- Manual Removal
- Chemical Removal
- Final Blow: Mega Mulch

Section 9:
PI Reader

Chapter 1:
Strange Facts and Terrible Tales ~ 109
- Japan: Dangerous Beauty and Mummified Monks
- Urishiol Around the Globe
- Cashews, Mangos and Toxic TreatsPoison Ivy and Europe
- Poison Ivy in Other Languages
- Native Americans, PI Masters – Not
- Poison Oak as Art
- Pop Culture Poison Ivy
- Poison Ivy, Batman's Nemesis

Chapter 2:
Debunking the Bull Manure ~ 115
- Stupid and Even Deadly Home Remedies
- Myth Busting

Resources

Bibliography ~ 121

Illustration and Photo Credits ~ 133

About the Author ~ 139

The Big Itchy Picture

Section Index
1. Poison Oak and Poison Ivy: Weirder Than You Know

itch

pronounce: iCH/

to have or produce an unpleasant feeling on your skin or inside your mouth, nose, etc. that makes you want to scratch

~ Mirriam-Webster definition

Lots of things can make you itch. Few create itches so horrendous that death seems like sweet relief. But poison oak and ivy sure can. The weeping blisters have all the pleasure of a napalm burn. The rash seems to spread and goes on for days, even weeks. Sleep is impossible.

Section 1 / Chapter 1

Poison Oak and Poison Ivy: Weirder Than You Know

Chapter Index
- The Rash and You
- The Stages of PI Rash
- When it Comes to PI, it's Personal

I feel your pain. Since you are reading this book, chances are you are suffering from a rash created by exposure to poison oak or ivy (abbreviated in *Itchy Business* as PI). I am a pale, pink person with thin delicate skin. The plant thinks my body is an amusement park. Learn from my horrible, horrible experience.

For over five decades, I have been a walking laboratory for PI. As a lover of the outdoors, I faced occasional accidental exposure. Once I went into wildlife habitat rehabilitation, I had to encounter PI all the time. Like farm and ranch workers, forestry crews, landscapers, and others in outdoor occupations, I didn't have the luxury of avoiding the plant. I had to become a PI ninja and overcome it with my wits.

> The abbreviation "PI" refers to both poison oak and poison ivy.

The Rash & You

PI provokes one of the most common skin allergies in the United States. The American Academy of Dermatology estimates up to 50 million people are afflicted a year. Sufferers erupt in patches of swelling and inflammation that bloom into a red, raw rash. Blisters weep copiously and create an ugly crust of dried goo. The itch ranges from merely awful to delirium producing, and the rash persists for one to two weeks, sometimes longer.

Allergic dermatitis from PI accounts for ten percent of lost-time injuries by U.S. Forest Service employees. In the poison oak territory of California, Oregon, and Washington, encounters with the plant disable one-third of forestry workers each fire season. PI-related illnesses of agricultural, landscaping, timber and other outdoor workers make up about one percent of the workers' compensation claim budget in California.

Weird and contradictory, PI is abundant with metaphor and meaning:

- Neither oak nor ivy, PI consists of four species in the genus *Toxicodendron* that can manifest as a vine, shrub or even a tree.
- PI does not cause a contact rash. Instead it's an extreme allergic reaction that happens deep within the skin.
- Urushiol [oo-roo-**shee**-ohl], the allergen in PI, is so concentrated and toxic that a tablespoon microscopically dispersed could cause a rash in almost every person alive.
- The more firmly PI touches your skin, the sooner and more severely it will manifest in a rash. Light touches take longer, which is why the rash seems to spread.
- Humans are the only animals that are allergic to PI and our activities have created more places for it to flourish. Karmic, eh?

PI is confounding, even infuriating, because it is so variable. From 15 to 50 percent of people are not allergic to PI. Or at least not to small amounts. Or only after they'd taken a bath. Or just in the spring and not in the fall. Anyone can become allergic to PI at any time. Or become immune. It's simply perverse.

Respond to the PI rash like there's a poison to be neutralized and you'll worsen it and damage the skin. Approach the rash like an allergy to be managed and sweet rapid relief is yours. Because by the time the rash is rolling, the "poison" urushiol no longer exists. More on the human body's fascinating overkill allergic reaction in the Rash Mastery section.

By reading *Itchy Business* you can learn how to:

- Identify PI in all seasons and regions
- Clean PI off your skin, even hours past exposure
- Catch the PI rash early on and stop it in its tracks
- Greatly minimize the rash by managing it in stages
- Eradicate PI by heating and smothering its root system

You'll learn how to master the Cs of itch relief -- calm, cool, and constrict -- and how to practice safe scratch. *Itchy Business* includes tested holistic remedies and sifts out the ghastly, even dangerous, home remedies from the effective ones. You will be surprised at the myriad of inexpensive and effective options available to treat the PI rash.

The Stages of Rash

The first step is to get as much urushiol out of your skin as possible. Once the rash is on, it goes through stages and each requires a different management approach. You have to move fast! Once the PI rash gets going, it has a LOT of momentum. It's on a rampage, pure and simple.

Stage 1: Interrupt the Rash
Stage 2: Master the Itch
Stage 3: Manage the Blisters
Stage 4: Heal the Skin

Much of how your body responds to PI depends on the state of your immune system. The severity of the rash also varies by how firmly you contacted PI, how quickly you washed it off, and your body's particular state that day. Exposure worsens when the weather's hot, as does the rash.

> For information on PI in the news and updates on products, please visit the book website:
> WWW.ITCHY.BIZ

Key to all stages is a mental shift. You must become a PI ninja. Being very aware of your surroundings is key to avoiding PI exposure. By intently observing the body's reactions to exposure, you can detect the crucial pre-rash stage. Once the rash is on its rampage, you must engage it like a martial artist does a larger opponent by deflecting and guiding its momentum. PI is our Zen teacher.

With the right attitude, products and practices for each stage, you can become a PI master. If you're outdoors a lot, it's wise to read the entire *Itchy Business*. If you're suffering right now, go directly to the Rash Remedies section. Determine what stage your rash is in and follow that treatment. Once healed, read the other sections so you won't be miserable from PI again.

When it Comes to PI, it's Personal

Captain John Smith a few days after encountering poison ivy.

The name poison ivy came from British explorer Captain John Smith, who in 1609 wrote (in so many words) "What the #&%* is this?!" Yet the rest of nature loves it. Lots of berries for birds and small critters, lush high-protein leaves for deer and rabbit browsing, terrific root system for erosion control along creeks and bodies of water. The vines offer shelter for arboreal creatures. Except for making us miserable, it's a great plant.

Aside from a few small scantily furred primates, Homo sapiens are the only animals acutely sensitive to PI. As I reimagine our archetypal fall from Eden, God didn't punish humans by kicking us out of the garden. We kept the garden. God gave us PI instead. In some weird way, PI sensitivity is the human evolutionary fee for losing our fur, the price we pay for consciousness.

PI is our bane as Americans. The poison ivy species *Toxicodendron radicans* may be native to China, but sure found its happy place in the United States, spinning off three additional poison oak and ivy species. PI thrives on the edge of woods and open land. By carving roads and making clearings through the immense forest that once covered much of the U.S., we greatly multiplied its acreage.

There is no escaping PI. It thrives on the higher carbon dioxide levels involved with climate change. Hotter temperatures? PI says: "Bring it on!" Not only will it flourish in our polluted future, studies show it may become even more poisonous than it is now. Let the fruits of my struggles spare you from being a PI poster child. Learn PI mastery.

Fear nature no more!

PLEASE READ THESE CAUTIONS

Do you feel sick from the rash? You may need immediate medical attention. Read the chapter When To See a Doctor — Fast! in the Rash Mastery section.

If there are open cuts or lesions, broken skin or blisters, or otherwise abraded skin, be extra cautious with topical products.

Read labels carefully for contraindications.

Always consult with a physician first if you are pregnant or nursing, on medications or supplements, or have an acute or chronic health condition.

All topical products can cause contact dermatitis. If skin becomes additionally dry, red, inflamed or itchy, stop using the product.

If you have sensitive skin, test prior to use by applying to a small area first and monitoring for skin reactions.

Understanding Urushiol

Section Index
1. Urushiol, Your Foe
2. Cleaning Off Urushiol

Most rashes arise from encounters with substances that are caustic, corrosive, inflammatory or otherwise irritating to the skin and cause irritant contact dermatitis. The rash of poison oak and ivy (abbreviated in Itchy Business as PI) is not that. It is an allergic contact dermatitis, the most common in the nation. That allergen is urushiol [oo-roo-shee-ohl].

Only by understanding urushiol can you successfully prevent PI exposure, clean it off or heal the rash. Read on and discover who's allergic, who's not, and how that changes, and why some PI rashes are worse than others. Find out why de-sensitizing the body to urushiol is a fruitless task. Best of all, discover how to clean it off your skin so you don't get the rash.

Section 2 / Chapter 1

Urushiol, Your Foe

Chapter Index
- Understand the Allergen to Outwit It
- Who's Allergic, Who's Not, and How That Changes
- Levels of Misery: Why Some Rashes Are Worse Than Others
- No Such Luck: De-sensitizing the Body to Urushiol

Urushiol is essentially invisible. It takes forever to evaporate or disintegrate. A pinprick's worth is all it takes to provoke a PI rash in a sensitive person. It bonds quickly and deeply in the skin. The very definition of a "formidable opponent." Understanding the microscopic, molecular level that urushiol operates on is the first step to being a PI ninja.

Understand the Allergen to Outwit It

Urushiol is a force of nature, which makes PI one, too. A resin carries the heavy, yellowish oil via canals lacing the interior of PI and other Toxicodendrons. A single grain of table salt weighs about 60 micrograms. It takes only 20 micrograms of pure urushiol (extracted from the resin) to provoke a rash in a person sensitive to it. A few teaspoons of finely dispersed urushiol can make most people on Earth plenty miserable.

> The abbreviation "PI" refers to both poison oak and poison ivy.

From its top-most leaf to its deepest root, every part of PI (except flower pollen and nectar) is flush with the urushiol-laden resin. Lucky for us, those ultra fine resin canals have to be broken in order for urushiol to leak out. Unlucky for us, it doesn't take much, especially with tender spring leaves. Scuffed up by dirt, roots release a lot of urushiol.

As urushiol descends through the epidermis it encounters Langerhan's cells where it oxidizes and binds with a protein on the outer membranes. That act sends the immune system into an allergic panic. The alien intruder is dragged into the dermis and lymph system. Helper T-cells get involved, then caustic lymphokines, and finally killer T-cells and their bruiser buddies the macrophages. Inflammatory mediators fuel the riot down in the dermis. The result is cytotoxic devastation that oozes outward — the PI rash. More on this fascinating process in the Rash Mastery section.

The terpene oleoresin that carries urushiol is extremely sticky and persistent, drying to a dark shiny hardness. The term urushiol derives from *urushi* (漆), the Japanese word for lacquer that elite craftsmen tap from the urushiol-laden Chinese lacquer tree (*Toxicodendron vernicifluum*). The lacquer is praised for its deep black sheen in artworks, but is also used on ceremonial and display containers to protect their precious contents.

A non-volatile oil, urushiol takes an extremely long time to evaporate, sticking around for years, even decades. PI specimens a century old in botany collections have imparted a rash. Like an invisible smudge of honey, urushiol moves easily from your clothes or pet's fur to vehicles, doorknobs, and furnishings. Your tools and toys from last summer? Chances are urushiol is still there, waiting for you.

Fairly rare but ultra sneaky is water-born urushiol. Like we didn't have enough to worry about. Urushiol is slightly water-soluble. If a creek, river or lake bank is coated with PI, the adjacent water will have some, too. So will nearby soil that's muddy. Extended heavy rain on a lush PI patch can wash some urushiol downhill. Just awful.

Urushiol shows up in other unlikely places. Several other members of the cashew family contain an urushiol-like compound. Sensitive folks might get a rash from raw cashews or mango peel. More on undercover urushiol in the Strange Facts and Terrible Tales section.

> ### PLEASE READ THESE CAUTIONS
>
> Do you feel sick from the rash? You may need immediate medical attention. Read the chapter When To See a Doctor — Fast! in the Rash Mastery section.
>
> If there are open cuts or lesions, broken skin or blisters, or otherwise abraded skin, be extra cautious with topical products.
>
> Read labels carefully for contraindications.
>
> Always consult with a physician first if you are pregnant or nursing, on medications or supplements, or have an acute or chronic health condition.
>
> All topical products can cause contact dermatitis. If skin becomes additionally dry, red, inflamed or itchy, stop using the product.
>
> If you have sensitive skin, test prior to use by applying to a small area first and monitoring for skin reactions.

Who's Allergic, Who's Not, and How That Changes

Three out of four people are members of the PI Club. They react to urushiol to some degree in certain situations. At least one-quarter of the population is like me, virulently allergic. If your parents were PI sensitive, there's a big chance you will be, too. Only 10 to 15 percent of us won't react at all.

Folks who think they're immune to PI shouldn't get cocky about it though. Sensitivity to PI can happen at any time. So can non-reactivity. It all depends on the state of a person's immune system and that can vary throughout a life. So you can be more sensitive to PI as a child, but not as an adult, and vice versa. Repeated exposure to urushiol can make you less sensitive to it. It can also make you *more* sensitive.

Certain states of immune systems prevent the PI rash response. Some immune-mediated diseases like eczema can bring about PI immunity. HIV patients sometimes don't have enough immune system to react to it. Infants and folks over 60 rarely get the rash. Of course, they're outside less, too.

African Americans are said to be less prone to PI though some scientists dispute that. Hispanics and Native Americans react with the same virulence as Caucasians. Inuits don't seem to, but data is slim. Besides, how often does an arctic dweller come across PI anyway?

Levels of Misery: Why Some Rashes Are Worse Than Others

If the exposure to urushiol is light or limited, the rash will be, too. Sometimes it's not that people are immune to PI, but that everything lines up in their favor to minimize exposure and reactivity.

These things make for enhanced absorption of urushiol and a greater likelihood of a bad rash:

- A longer or firmer touch of the plant (more urushiol goes deeper into the dermis)
- Contact with young plants or tender growing leaves (easier for urushiol to escape)
- Thin skin such as the face, ears, anus and genitalia (oh no!)
- Recently washed skin (removes protective skin oils)
- Hot temperatures (opens skin pores)
- Sweat and sweaty clothes (slathers urushiol about)
- Bug bites, scratched skin, cuts or sores (entry to the dermis is swift and deep)
- Inhaling PI smoke (can seriously inflame the entire respiratory system and even kill you)

Basically, if you make firm contact with PI — grabbing it, leaning on it, falling on it, getting slapped by a stem — you've had serious exposure to urushiol.

These things make for less absorption of urushiol and milder rashes:
- A light touch of the plant (takes longer to seep in, better chance of getting washed off)
- Contact with older plants or tougher, late-season leaves (harder for urushiol to escape)
- Skin with an especially gnarly outer layer of epithelial cells (usually burly men)
- Thick skin such as the soles, palms or any place calloused (go epithelial cells!)
- Unwashed skin, or oily skin such as the nose or forehead (shiny is good)
- Hairy skin (we should never have let go of our fur)
- Cool temperatures (shrinks pores)

You can extend or worsen the rash in these ways:
- Secondary exposure from urushiol on your clothes, shoes, tools, equipment, and especially your pets (it's the gift that keeps on giving)
- Treating the rash by being brutal to your skin (be a PI rash ninja instead)
- Scratching and aggravating your skin so much it gets infected (PI ninjas don't do that)

The two best things you can do to avoid the rash or at least minimize it:
- Use a PI barrier cream on your skin (a must! — more in the Defending Yourself section)
- Wash exposed skin, clothing and objects after potential PI exposure (ditto! — more in Defending Yourself)

No Such Luck: De-sensitizing the Body to Urushiol

"My uncle made himself immune to poison ivy by eating the young leaves."

No, he didn't. He was rather cranky, yes? Now you know why. Think about it. The amount of urushiol on the head of a pin can incite a rash in thousands of people. So chewing on a leaf can do serious damage to your insides, especially tender mucous membranes, whether you're immediately aware of it or not.

You can't become immune to PI by drinking the milk of goats that forage on it — no urushiol remains in the milk. Or by eating honey made by bees who visit the flowers — there's no urushiol in nectar or pollen.

Pharmaceutical companies have tried to create PI rash prevention compounds using a variety of approaches. Limited success has been claimed, but side effects were horrid or the immunity was too temporary:
- Vaccine to block the specific T-cell receptor for urushiol
- Injection of suppressor T-cells to calm over-reactive T-cells
- IgG immunoglobulin antibodies to block the Langerhan's receptor
- De-sensitization using esterified urushiol or cyclodextrin-urushiol complexes

However, usushiol immunity can be done. Some people who've worked for decades with *urushi* from the Japanese lacquer tree, or who process cashew and mango peel containing a similar compound, have developed PI immunity.

For information on PI in the news and updates on products, please visit the book website:

WWW.ITCHY.BIZ

Section 2 / Chapter 2

Cleaning Off Urushiol

Chapter Index
- Exposure Timeline
- Within 5 minutes: Water
- Within an Hour: Detergent, Alcohol and Oxygen
- Within a Day: Solvents
- If the Rash Appears: Scrubs
- In the Field: What Not to Do
- Post-Cleaning Skin Care

"Oh no, I got some on me!" Bummer, but at least you know when and where exposure occurred. Most of the time we don't. Scientists are developing a special light detects urushiol [oo-roo-**shee-**ohl] by making it fluoresce. Hurry the heck up with that! Once in touch with poison oak and ivy (abbreviated in *Itchy Business* as PI), you are in a race against time. You must get as much out of your skin as soon as possible.

Exposure Timeline

If the contact with PI was firm, the skin thin and freshly washed, and the weather hot, the allergen might reach the inner epidermis in five hours. But if the contact was light, the skin thick and dirty, and the weather cool, it could take days.

Even catching exposure immediately may not remove all the usushiol. But it will reduce the amount and thus mute the rash unless you're highly sensitive. The longer the delay in cleaning, the stickier urushiol gets and the harder it is to remove, requiring stronger cleaners that can deeply penetrate the skin.

- Within 5 Minutes: Water
- From 5 Minutes to 2 Hours: Detergent, Alcohol or Oxygen
- From 2 Hours to 2 Days: Solvents
- Once the Rash Appears: Scrubs

Go straight to PI solvents if exposure to PI is firm, on thin skin, or if you are especially sensitive.

Be proactive. Wash all exposed skin after being outdoors in PI territory, regardless if you think you contacted it or not. If exposure was probable, clean your clothes and objects, too. More in the Defending Yourself section.

> The abbreviation "PI" refers to both poison oak and poison ivy.

Do everyone a favor and clean outside where urushiol-laden water can go directly into the ground. Or use a sink or container that can be emptied safely down the drain and then washed or tossed. Either way, afterwards clean the entire area where you washed up.

Keep in mind that after cleaning your skin is devoid of oils and much more vulnerable to PI exposure.

Within 5 Minutes: Water

If you're lucky, skin oils and hairs keep urushiol beaded on the surface for a while. The fresh resin picks up and moves quickly in water, especially oxygenated flowing water. Don't use soap — you want the microscopic blobs of resin to roll off rather than diffuse.

Rinse profusely with water in a slow to moderate stream (not gushing) and at an angle (not pressing directly into the skin). Too little water and you risk spreading the urushiol around. Cool to lukewarm is optimum. Hot water opens the pores. Very cold may cause you to you skimp on washing. Creek and other natural water work fine. If no water is available, use whatever liquid you've got, even soda drinks.

Within an Hour: Detergent, Alcohol and Oxygen

Detergent

Once the urushiol begins sinking into the skin, serious cleaning power is needed. Don't use soap of any kind. Period. Not even Fels-Naptha, which is no longer the same one your grandma used anyway. Or any soap pitched as being for PI; those are best for soothing a rash. No scrubs either.

A strong dishwashing detergent is required, one with lots of surfactant. It must make a profuse amount of suds. Surfactants keep molecules like urushiol from re-depositing on the skin. Very important! Avoid detergents with added emollients. Look for ones with a de-greasing agent or oxygen power, often called a bleach alternative. Foaming versions add oomph and are easier to use.

Use lots and lots of water and wash for minutes at a time. Scrub thoroughly with a washcloth or sponge. If you have no water available, an acceptable substitute are waterless hand cleaners used by mechanics.

Whatever detergent you use, if exposure to PI was firm do a final brisk rub with isopropyl (rubbing) alcohol to try and remove urushiol from deeper in the epidermis.

> Items listed are not endorsements, but used only to demonstrate the types of products available.

Fels-Naptha by Purex/Dial Corp.
- No. Just no. When Fels and Co. created the tallow-based laundry bar soap in 1893, it was the first to include naphtha or Stoddard solvent, a petroleum refining byproduct that was used in dry cleaning. But it doesn't contain naptha anymore, making it useless as a PI cleaner.

Goop Hand Cleaner
- Thick cream favored by mechanics to remove grease. Orange Goop is a lightweight gel with a nice smell. Available in several formats, including pre-moistened towels that are very handy for wiping down dogs and tools.

Ivarest Medicated Poison Ivy Cleansing Formula
- Effective high-suds soap with menthol, better as a rash treatment.

Ultra Dishwashing Liquid or **Direct Dishwashing Foam Pump** by Dawn
- Super powerful, yet safe enough to use on oil-covered seabirds.

Ultra Oxy Plus Power Degreaser by Palmolive
- A serious contender.

Alcohol

Isopropyl or rubbing alcohol cuts the stickiness of fresh urushiol and helps move it out. A 70% solution is the most common, but 90% and up exists, albeit a bit tough on the skin. Being only 40% ethyl (drinking) alcohol, vodka and other liquors are not much better than water. Hand sanitizer gel is 50 to 70% ethyl alcohol and will do if you're lacking isopropyl or PI solvents. A pre-moistened alcohol wipe is too likely to press the urushiol into the skin.

Once you've rinsed for a minute or so, alternate with brisk scrubbing sessions of isopropyl soaked cotton or cloth.

Syringe Method
- Get as large a needle-less syringe as you can; 1 mm/100 cc is a good size. Mine came from the vet. A baster will also work. Rinse exposed body part firmly without splashing.

Drip Method
- Fill a bowl with rubbing alcohol. Scoop or sponge up some alcohol and let it drain over the exposed body part. Don't let it drip back into the bowl.

Container Method
- Stuff a canning jar or other well-sealed glass container with cotton balls or squares of cotton rags or diapers (clean, of course) and fill with alcohol. Squeeze over the rash. Good to keep a jar around when you're away from civilization.

Oxygen

As a phenolic compound, urushiol may be destabilized by interactions with oxygen. The theory goes that using oxygenated water could remove urushiol effectively, though it still has to penetrate the epidermis. No proof, but worth a try, especially if you don't know anyone who could blast you with oxygen from an oxyacetylene cutting torch (just kidding about that).

- Make a weak solution of OxiClean Stain Remover.
- Create a mix of 1 or 2 parts hydrogen peroxide to 1 part water.
- Use a 10% bleach solution by adding ¼ cup to 2 ½ to 3 cups of water.

Pour over the rash site, then alternate with scrubbing sessions. Keep these oxygenated waters well away from the eyes, private parts, and all mucous membranes as well as fabrics and objects. If contact is made, flush with plain water for 15 minutes and consult a doctor. Use only in a well-ventilated area.

Do not wash with oxygen and then use a solvent such as Tecnu or a scrub like Zanfel. Do not use oxygen products in conjunction with strong acids or alkalines.

Oxygen Bleach Plus by biokleen
- Hydrogen peroxide and sodium carbonate zinged by grapefruit seed extract and softened by glycerin.

Versatile Stain Remover Free or **Baby Stain Soaker** by OxiClean
- The household oxygen pioneer, using sodium carbonate and sodium percarbonate powder in water to create a high-oxygen solution. These versions are additive free.

In a pinch, you can use some of the oxygen creams listed in the Rash Remedies section. Apply, rub vigorously, rinse, repeat.

Within a Day: Solvents

After an hour or so, it's time for PI solvents. These liquid petroleum products penetrate deeper into skin and are paired with high-powered surfactants that move the urushiol up and out. Often fatty acids are added to help counter the extreme drying that solvents cause. Thankfully, they're deodorized or given cover aromas.

PI solvents are worth trying hours, even days, after exposure. Firmer touches of PI manifest into a rash first, so you can be fairly sure there's more to arise. A last-chance dash to remove nearby unbonded urushiol may not get it all, but sure will scare the heck out of it.

Don't use PI solvents after the rash blooms. Pouring solvents in open wounds is bad for your health and may lead to scarring. Not for use after cleaning with oxygen and wait a few days before applying hydrocortisone ointments.

Rub PI solvents briskly into the skin with a washcloth or sponge for two to three minutes. Wash off with plenty of water and repeat again and again. PI solvents can be very hard on the skin and increase potential for PI exposure for a day or so after use.

Ivy Off by Ivy Off
- An interesting two-step process. A clear solvent gel is rubbed into the skin and then washed off with an accompanying high-surfactant soap. Available online.

Ivy X Post-Contact Skin Cleanser by CoreTex
- A strong solvent-surfactant combo with chamomile, calendula, green tea, and white oak extracts for skin healing. Comes in a variety of sizes and formats. Available online and at most agricultural and outdoor stores, often sold direct to outdoor industries.

Tecnu Outdoor Skin Cleanser by Tec Labs
- The best-selling PI solvent-surfactant combo is well loved and rightly so. It rocks, a lifesaver for many people. Available online and at most drug, agricultural and outdoor stores. Comes in a variety of sizes and formats.

If the Rash Appears: Scrubs

Sometimes a rash is the first hint you encountered PI. Take cleaning a step further with PI scrubs: detergent containing teeny exfoliating beads that enable strong surfactants to penetrate deeper into the skin and lift urushiol away. (Don't use typical cosmetic exfoliants — too abrasive and not enough surfactant.) PI scrubs can be pricey. But sweet mother of God, the itch relief! I proposed marriage to Zanfel once.

PI scrubs are not for use after lesions open or blisters appear. They leave minute abrasions on the skin that can make it quite painful to use anti-itch analgesics and cooling potions containing camphor, menthol or aromatic herbs, greatly limiting your treatment options.

Extreme Poison Ivy Medicated Scrub by Tecnu
- With grindelia to help with itch and inflammation.

büji Wash by büji
- Hypoallergenic, dye and fragrance free.

Zanfel Poison Ivy, Oak & Sumac Wash
- The best-selling original. Nice company that does good deeds.

If you're aware enough to catch the initial stage of the PI rash — hot, mottled, swollen skin — you can try to interrupt the rash. More on that in Stage 1 in the Rash Remedies section.

> For information on PI in the news and updates on products, please visit the book website:
> WWW.ITCHY.BIZ

In the Field: What Not to Do

Be a PI ninja by wearing the right clothes and applying special urushiol barrier creams before heading out into PI territory. Always carry water. Take portable alcohol and solvent cleaners. More in the Defending Yourself section.

If you get PI exposure without your ninja tools and you're unable to hustle back for a proper cleaning, there's little you can do. Do not rub your skin with bark, leaves or (heaven forbid) dirt. Urushiol operates on a molecular level. Any firm contact at all will press urushiol deep into the skin and miniscule incisions caused by dirt make it far worse.

Your last-chance option is absorption if you move immediately. *Do this only if desperate.*

- Leaves, preferably downy or fuzzy: Hovering a hair's width above the skin, daub (do not wipe) with a leaf in an attempt to lift off the urushiol resin.
- Clay: Light powdery clay like bentonite dusted on the exposed skin might help absorb the urushiol. But if you remember to pack bentonite, why not take barrier creams and cleaners?

Post-Cleaning Skin Care

Washing with detergent, alcohol or oxygenated water, as well as solvents and scrubs, dry out and even strafe your skin. This makes further urushiol absorption easier and may also lead to increased PI and sunlight sensitivity. Dry skin makes any PI rash that may arise far itchier.

Take care of your skin after cleaning to help counter these effects. Details in Stage 4 of the Rash Remedies section. Wait an hour or two to allow pores to close and the skin's acid mantle to restore.

Rash Mastery

Section Index
1. Rash 101
2. It's All About That Itch
3. When the Rash Goes Bad

Mastery of the PI rash means understanding it on a deep level. The first rule of being a PI ninja: Know your opponent. The core philosophy of PI ninjahood is imparted in this section, along with:

- The structure of the skin, what the components are, and what they do.
- The cellular immune-system reactions that create the rash response to urushiol.
- The science of itch and how you can manipulate it to work in your favor.

While warriors must prepare for success, sometimes it eludes us, so you must be able to recognize when the rash has gone very, very bad. That is covered, too.

Section 3 / Chapter 1

Rash 101

Chapter Index
- The Skin: First Line of Defense
- Mob Mentality: How Allergic Overreaction Creates the Rash

To master the rash of poison oak and ivy (abbreviated in Itchy Business as PI), you have to be aware of the skin's complex structure and its role in the immune system. The skin is the body's largest organ, about ten percent of our weight, and serves as the first line of defense against all invaders.

The Skin: First Line of Defense

The skin has three main layers:
- Epidermis and acid mantle — outer
- Dermis — middle
- Subcutaneous tissue — inner

Subcutaneous Tissue

The lowest skin layer consists of fatty tissue and separates the dermis from underlying muscles.
- This tissue throbs with blood vessels: veins, arteries, and the capillaries that connect them.
- Lymph system conduits run more or less parallel to those, carrying a clear beneficial fluid that bathes tissues. Part of the immune system, it mainly comes to mind when the lymph glands that secrete it get swollen during bad infections.
- The bases of hair follicles, sweat glands, sebaceous glands, and nerves reside here.

> Do you feel sick from the rash? You may need immediate medical attention. Read the chapter When To See a Doctor – Fast! in this section.

Dermis

The dermis is the juicy collagen-rich part of skin, alive with activity.
- Pathogen and allergen-seeking cells of the immune system. You know some as T-cells. These guys go wild in a PI allergic reaction.
- Nerve tips or fibrils specialized to transmit messages of various kinds, including pain and itch.

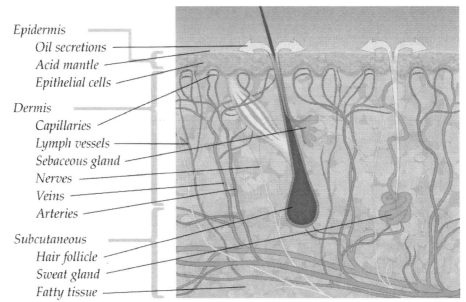

Epidermis
  Oil secretions
  Acid mantle
  Epithelial cells
Dermis
  Capillaries
  Lymph vessels
  Sebaceous gland
  Nerves
  Veins
  Arteries
Subcutaneous
  Hair follicle
  Sweat gland
  Fatty tissue

Layers of the Skin

Epidermis

The exterior layer of the epidermis consists of microscopic layers of dead cells pushed out by the dermis below.

- Epithelial cells and their lively acid-mantle ecosystem of beneficial skin bacteria and fatty acids are a crucial defense against PI.
- Beneath those epithelial cells is the first live and juicy layer of the skin. It contains a type of cell called Langerhan's that causes all kinds of trouble when it encounters urushiol.

Acid Mantle

A protective invisible viscous film called the acid mantle coats the epidermis. Sebaceous glands secrete oily sebum, and eccrine sweat glands release lactic and amino acids. Mixed with dead epithelial cells, it's like a snack feast for hungry micro beasts. Their waste products create our fine mammalian stink. Acid mantle pH for skin usually ranges from 4.5 to 5.5. If the skin becomes too acidic or alkaline, its natural flora can't function. If the skin becomes too alkaline, it's more susceptible to infections.

Mob Mentality: How Allergic Overreaction Creates the Rash

Most people don't react to their first encounter with PI unless they're ultra susceptible. In this initial sensitization phase, Langerhan's cells take in information (hmmm, it's that urushiol), review it (urushiol bad!) and pass it on to T-lymphocytes, who spread the word throughout the body with vigilante fervor.

The abbreviation "PI" refers to both poison oak and poison ivy.

The body isn't just allergic to urushiol. It's psychotic about it. This poor allergen tourist is treated like it's a terrorist. Immune cells come to an irrational conclusion (urushiol is a huge threat!), make maniacal plans (must exterminate urushiol!), and stand on point ready to call out the body's mob of cellular assassins. That process usually happens by age 14.

If a person doesn't encounter PI again, or never touches it all or at least not until adulthood, they may never develop an allergy to it. That's why PI immunity rates among highly urban folks are higher than rural, yet their need for immunity is less. See what I mean about PI being perverse?

With subsequent exposure, called the elicitation phase, urushiol descends through the epidermis and encounters Langerhan's and other antigen-presenting cells. The alarm is sounded! Urushiol oxidizes and binds with a protein on the outer membranes.

Langerhan's and its pals transport the urushiol into the dermis' regional lymph nodes. The immune system views the transformed urushiol as a major alien threat. A red alert resonates throughout the immune system.

Effector T-cells, a type of helper T-cells, are first on the scene (must stop this threat!). Millions patrol our blood and lymph, programmed to look for specific allergens like urushiol. The effector T-cells send in caustic lymphokines that mob the urushiol (come on team, kill the enemy!).

This rampage excites the gangster cousins, the killer T-cells, and their hungry pals, the macrophages. These big bruising cells, the linebackers of the immune system, damage blood vessels when they rush en masse to storm the urushiol.

With their big guns full of toxins, killer T-cells blast away at urushiol (die, allergen, die!) and everything near it, causing intense collateral damage. A gang of white blood cells, including gnarly mast cells, release inflammatory mediators like histamine, leukotriene, and prostaglandins that fuel the riot (burn, baby, burn!).

This fiery T-cell mediated immune response results in cytotoxic devastation — the PI rash. The nice guys, regulatory T-cells, finally saunter in and cool things down. The immune system goes back to its usual business, leaving behind a ravaged battlefield — your skin.

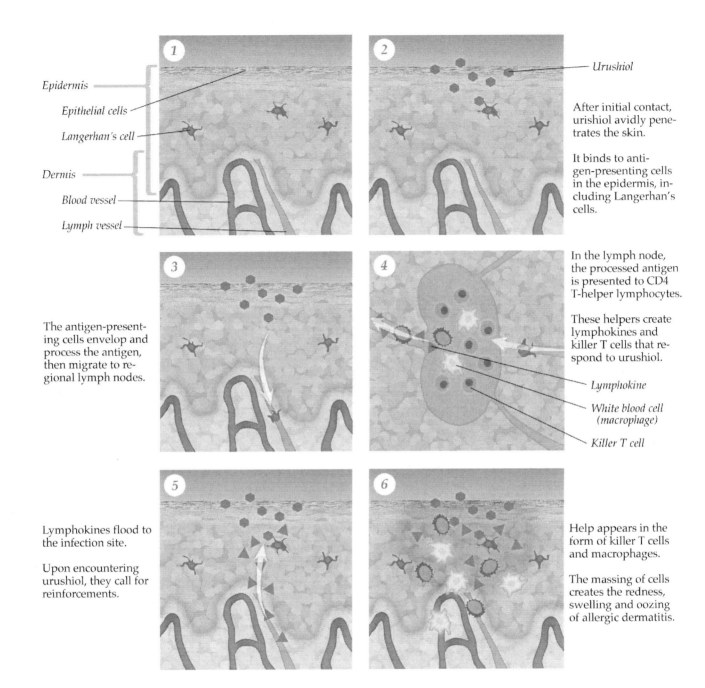

Allergic Contact Dermatitis

Section 3 / Chapter 2

It's All About That Itch

Chapter Index
- What Is Itch?
- Be a PI Ninja
- Transcend the Itch
- Holistic: For the Long Run

Deal with the itchiness of the poison oak and ivy (abbreviated in *Itchy Business* as PI) as you would a cranky child. Let it know you recognize that it is upset, do your best to calm and cool it down, and then distract it while setting a few limits. You have to be the adult. It's not easy.

What Is Itch?

Itch is a distress signal sent by nerves. It is your body's way of saying "Get that %!#* thing out of here." Scratching is how you obey the body.

The itchy eyes and nose of hay fever are prompted by mast cells releasing histamine. The irritation and inflammation of a simple contact rash can kick up quite an itch. Dying is itchy business, making cell death or necrosis another itch producer. Even very dry skin can cause itch.

The PI itch uses different neural pathways, so techniques for those itchy maladies tend to not be effective on the rash. For lack of a better term, PI itch is more "nervy," more like pain.

The sensation of scratching trumps the sensation of itch, overwhelming the nerves. Sort of stuns them for while. It's like the bright

> The abbreviation "PI" refers to both poison oak and poison ivy.

shiny object trick with a crying toddler, getting the nerves to pay attention to something else for a while. Learning how to make the most of that momentary confusion is the key to itch relief, PI ninja style.

> Do you feel sick from the rash? You may need immediate medical attention. Read the chapter When to See a Doctor – Fast! in this section.

When the itch is scratched, soothed or distracted, the brain gets the idea that that the job was done. Once things calm down and the nerves check in again, they realize they'd been fooled — the itch was still there! The process starts all over.

It is easy to get on your nerves' nerves. Too much scratching and too many harsh PI products make the itch twitchy, setting up a tit-for-tat downward spiral that ends in infection. With a PI rash your skin nerves are literally fried. Be nice to them.

Be a PI Ninja

The typical doctor and drugstore way of dealing with PI itch is very direct: either shut it down with steroids or chemically bludgeon it into submission with analgesics. All too often the cost is Pyrrhic for your skin and makes you more susceptible to PI down the line.

Resistance is futile. As an opponent, PI is far stronger than any of us, its weapon is bigger than anything we've got. You don't want to win the battle yet lose the war. So you have to be a PI ninja and outwit the rash. You are capable of being nimble and creative. The rash is not.

Like in kung fu, you are taking the incredible hardwired, direct cellular momentum of the PI allergic reaction, channeling its energy, and deflecting it outward. In that opportune moment of weakness, you move in and calm the core of the problem: inflammation.

Now that the rash is less reactive, the PI ninja further cools and constricts it, dampening its momentum, in the process subduing and shortening its response. A ninja manages the rash, rather than the rash managing you.

Think Zen; act martial arts. Be smart, not muscular. Be stealthy, not direct. Be determined, not angry. Be cooperative, not confrontational. Be fast, precise and intense. Expend the minimal amount of energy for the greatest results.

Above all, don't panic. The PI rash response is made worse on all levels by reactiveness, physical as well as mental. Do not react. Act instead.

Transcend the Itch

In the PI rash, you are going to itch almost non-stop for several days. It might itch a little; it might itch a lot. But it will be your surly houseguest for quite a while. You must learn to co-exist with itch.

Living with itch is a lot like living with pain. You have to establish who's the boss: you or the pain or itch. If you don't, that itch will own you. You become your itch's bitch.

You need to acknowledge the itch, without giving into it, without dismissing its need for attention. But give it limits, restricting what it will get from you. You establish a relationship with your itch. Just like you would a child.

And you have to accept the itch. Railing at it won't make it go away. It's a serious mental shift to submit to the inevitable and not collapse into it, but instead embrace it. If you have made peace with death, you can make peace with PI. If you have not, a PI rash is a good time to tackle the Big D. It's karmic, man.

Some suggestions:
- Stay calm. Do not worry.
- Practice meditation, tai chi or yoga.
- Think cooling thoughts. Release anger.
- Hypnosis to calm the body's reactiveness could help.
- Drink relaxing herb teas like chamomile and passionflower.
- Remember that it's temporary and in a few days it will be over.
- If all else fails, consider tranquilizers or anti-anxiety herbal supplements.

Hypnotic suggestion can help calm nervous reactiveness, relieve anxiety, and reduce stress over the PI rash. Use the power of your mind to persuade your immune system to respond in a more sane fashion. Everybody chill.

Most hypnotherapists use guided meditation to usher a patient into a deep meditative or trance state so that suggestions can be imparted to the patient's subconscious. The session is often recorded so that it can be repeated at home. The entire process usually takes an hour.

Locate a hypnotherapist near you: www.hypnosis.edu/hypnotherapists/search

Holistic: For the Long Run

PI ninja attitude jives well with the holistic mind-frame of getting at the root of the problem instead of reacting to symptoms.

Rather than deadening the itch with lidocaine or strafing it into submission with harsh counter-irritants, holistic stresses confusing itchy nerve endings with moderate heat, cold, acids or alkalines. Mind-body techniques impart a greater sense of control over the rash

The other Cs of itch mastery are: calm, cool, and constrict. Soothing herbs like calendula, grindelia, and plantain calm the riot going down in the dermis. Herbal aromatics such as camphor and menthol cool the rash. Astringents including witch hazel constrict the swelling.

But holistic is more than skin deep. The PI rash involves the whole body, extending well beyond the nastiness you see. Vitamins, supplements, and diet can calm the allergic response, boost the immune system, and reduce inflammation — working from the inside out.

Specific details on the holistic approach to PI rash are in the Rash Remedies section, in the chapter Holistic Techniques: Treat the Body, Reduce the Rash.

For information on PI in the news and updates on products, please visit the book website:

WWW.ITCHY.BIZ

Section 3 / Chapter 3

When the Rash Goes Bad

Chapter Index
- When to See a Doctor – Fast!
- What a Doctor Can Do
- Speaking Derma-Doc Talk
- The Hell of Inhalation

Most times we can endure the rash of poison oak and ivy (abbreviated in Itchy Business as PI). But there are some places on the body where a bad case should send you running to a doctor. The rash can easily get infected. And sometimes PI is more than a nasty rash. It can become a whole-bodied systemic affair, with urushiol [oo-roo-shee-ohl] wrecking havoc on tender interior tissues.

When to See a Doctor – Fast!

If you get a rash within a few hours of exposure, if your eyes or ears swell shut, or your throat feels constricted.
- You are highly sensitive and may be headed toward a severe, and possibly life threatening, allergic reaction.

If the rash is in the eyes, ears, nose or mouth, or on the genitals.
- These tender tissues allow urushiol to easily enter the dermis and lymph system, enabling it to bloom from simple inflammation to horrid illness in just a few hours.

If rash covers more than 10 to 20% of the body.
- You are in serious trouble. A rash that big can jack with your immune system, make you quite ill, and place you at great risk of serious infection.

If the rash appears several days afterward in places far from the original contact.
- It has triggered neural dermatitis and is awakening the site of every bad rash you ever had. That just sucks. It will pass, but oral steroids could help.

If you develop a high (100 degrees and up) temperature, become nauseated, get sore joints or the chills.
- The rash has gone systemic and urushiol has the entire lymph and immune system in an uproar. You are in a world of trouble. Seek help now.

If you feel an itch or heat in the throat or have difficulty breathing.
- You may have inhaled urushiol. Get immediate medical help. More in The Hell of Inhalation, below.

If you develop swelling (edema) in the ankles or other non-rash places.
- Severe or repeated rashes can cause nephritis or inflammation of the kidneys, caused by a build up of PI antibodies. This is very serious and potentially fatal.

If black spots on the skin persist.
- In black-spot poison ivy dermatitis, a dollop of urushiol is so significant that it reacts with the air and forms a black lacquer on the skin. Underneath it the allergic reaction is going ballistic from prolonged urushiol exposure.

What a Doctor Can Do
- Steroids, Oral
- Steroids, Prescription Strength Cream
- Antibiotics
- Withdraw Fluid From Blisters
- Mild Tranquilizer or Sleeping Aid
- Steroids: Relief at a Price

Steroids, Oral

If the rash is extensive, in a difficult place to treat, has extremely weepy blisters, or is infected, oral prescription steroids may be needed. A hefty dose of steroids (either as a shot or pills) is given to stop the rash reaction. It can be a huge relief! But it's a shock to the system. You must taper off with slowly decreasing dosages over a week or the rash will return. It's often prescribed in a handy properly dosed pack.

Steroids, Prescription Strength Cream

The butt and backs of thighs are almost constantly in contact with other surfaces, making rashes there difficult to heal. Same with the constant movement of rashes on the joints. Prescription strength steroid creams can greatly speed up the healing process. Over-the-counter topical corticosteroid creams are too weak. But strong topical steroids can mask signs of skin infection. The top layers may be healing while an infection rages beneath. Keep alert for pus, tenderness or heat, and read Steroids: Relief at a Price, below.

Antibiotics

Scratching the rash with your fingers enables the legions of bacteria on your hands and under your nails to penetrate deeply into the skin. Infection ensues. It can be a big issue in the blistery Stage 3.

Withdraw Fluid from Blisters

If the blisters become painfully large, a doctor can withdraw some of the fluid with a needle and apply a preventative antibiotic.

Mild Tranquilizer or Sleeping Aid

Really, you'll be amazed at how much it will help in Stages 2 and 3! It's hard to go to sleep while going mad from the itch.

Steroids: Relief at a Price

Oral corticosteroids, or steroids, work because they suppress the immune system and curtail the rash response. Of course, immune suppression leaves you wide open to other infections. The side effects of oral steroids fill pages and pages of medical texts. Big risks like adrenal suppression, glaucoma, high glucose, ulcers, edema, and high blood pressure.

Steroids can give some people gnarly insomnia, mania and seriously weird anxiety, if not psychosis. Irritating qualities include acne, fatigue, bloating and weight gain. Some steroids are easier on the mind and body than others. Ask your doctor for newer versions with fewer side effects.

Read and obey all product label warnings. Don't stop abruptly before the run of steroids is through. The rash may rebound or, worse, your adrenal glands may go haywire. It's not pretty. Take precautions and monitor carefully.

Speaking Derma-Doc Talk

When doctors talk rash, they use these terms:

- **antigen** = allergic substance (aka urushiol)
- **bulla** = blister or vesicle larger than 3/16 inch
- **dermis** = inner layer of skin
- **dermatitis** = rash
- **contact dermatitis** = caused by contact with a substance
- **acute contact dermatitis** or **ACD** = bad rash
- **allergen contact dermatitis** = caused by an allergen
- **irritant contact dermatitis** = caused by an irritant
- **plant contact dermatitis** = caused by a plant
- **epidermis** = outer layer of skin
- **erythematous** = redness of the skin caused by capillary congestion
- **inflammation** = first response of the immune system to allergy, infection or irritation, noted by redness, swelling and heat
- **papule** = small, solid, inflammatory eleva-

tion of the skin
- **pruritis** = itching
- **vesicle** = small serum-filled blister formed in or beneath the skin

The Hell of Inhalation

It might be as small as PI vines in hidden in firewood bark. Or as large as a forest fire of PI-laden trees. Even though nonvolatile, urushiol heats and splatters onto millions of teeny — even invisible — soot particles.

Urushiol-laden smoke on exposed skin can cause a rash and temporary blindness if it gets in the eyes. Inhaled PI easily goes systemic, with a body-wide rash, fever, chills, nausea and more — you are seriously ill. Hospitalization may be required.

Inhaling urushiol will cause extreme irritation to the respiratory tract, and the coughing is excruciatingly painful. Swelling can occur in the lungs, throat and nasal passages. Sometimes it's fatal — no air can penetrate at all.

This misery is inflicted on forest and prairie firefighters all too often. But unwary folks who burn brush piles and enjoy campfires can also suffer. Always stay away from bonfire smoke and remain well upwind of wildfires. If you must be around it, wear a respiratory mask rated for oily or toxic particulates, not just the usual dust mask.

For information on PI in the news and updates on products, please visit the book website:

WWW.ITCHY.BIZ

Your Rash Toolkit

Section Index
1. Practice Safe Scratch
2. The Stages: Your Key To Rash Relief
3. The Cs of Itch Relief
4. Plants and Minerals for Rash

You now know all about your opponent, poison oak and ivy (abbreviated in Itchy Business as PI), and its powerful weapon, urushiol [oo-roo-shee-ohl]. To complete your PI ninja training you need tools. It's time to suit up.

In this section, learn how to scratch safely by confusing the itch. Plan your mastery of the poison oak and ivy rash through deep knowledge of the four stages it goes through. Discover how the science of itch relief manifests in the three Cs: calm, cool, and constrict. A plethora of powerful plants and minerals, and how to use them, completes your tools.

Section 4 / Chapter 1

Practice Safe Scratch

Chapter Index
- Soft Friction
- Extreme Heat
- Extreme Cold
- Acids and Alkalines
- Counter-irritants
- Food Enzymes
- Night Gloves

Confuse your itch! Scratching simply serves to provide a sensation that overwhelms itch and gives your nerves something else to think about to for a while. Squirrel! The trick is to do it without using your fingernails. You can confuse an itch in a myriad of ways: extreme cold or heat, strong acids and alkalines, an array of counter-irritants, and even food enzymes.

If you practice safe scratch and don't damage your skin, use the quiet, itch-free period afterward to apply rash treatments. But don't get freaked out if you nick a blister and serum comes out. There's no urushiol [oo-roo-**shee**-ohl] in it.

Soft Friction

These methods impart a counter sensation without causing skin damage and worsening the rash. Relief tends to be relatively short term, from several minutes to an hour or so.
- Scratch around the rash with a rough washcloth.
- Tap on the rash lightly or use the palm of the hand to rub.
- Lay a rough, preferably damp and very warm, washcloth on top of the rash. Alternate between pressing down firmly and barely moving it back and forth.
- Wear a long-sleeved shirt in a knit or pebbled texture and do the technique above. So helpful when you have itchy arms at the office.
- Take a hairbrush and press gently into the rash in a rolling motion. Preferably a brush with rounded ends, but sharp bristles can be just the trick for an intense itch. The key is to avoid pressing deeply or dragging the tines across the skin.

PLEASE READ THESE CAUTIONS

Do you feel sick from the rash? You may need immediate medical attention. Read the chapter When To See a Doctor — Fast! in the Rash Mastery section.

If there are open cuts or lesions, broken skin or blisters, or otherwise abraded skin, be extra cautious with topical products.

Read labels carefully for contraindications.

Always consult with a physician first if you are pregnant or nursing, on medications or supplements, or have an acute or chronic health condition.

All topical products can cause contact dermatitis. If skin becomes additionally dry, red, inflamed or itchy, stop using the product.

If you have sensitive skin, test prior to use by applying to a small area first and monitoring for skin reactions.

Extreme Heat

Running hot water or blowing hot air over the rash releases a rush of itchiness for a few seconds that feels like the shortest, most intense, orgasm ever. For a few hours after, there's no itch at all. But heat releases copious amounts of inflammatory mediators that extend and often worsen the rash. Nasty infections can arise that make the rash exponentially more miserable, and antibiotics and steroids are often required, adding to the misery. So lean on it only as a last resort, like getting a few blessed itch-free hours to sleep.

> For more on the PI rash process, see the prior Rash Mastery section. Products and practices for rash relief are in the next section, Rash Remedies.

Here's a theory of how it works. Mast cells are white blood cells covered with teeny poles or masts that contain neurotransmitters like histamine. Usually these dribble out. The idea is that heat causes those masts to unleash their load all at once and peace reigns while their chemicals restore.

Once a couple of masts begin releasing histamine in earnest, little additional prompting is needed to make the whole cell blow. You only need to start that chain reaction. So it's possible to get that extreme relief without worsening the rash. Think tantric. Start slow, increase right to the point of climax, and pull back. Repeat until you feel the Big O coming on and quickly get out of the heat. Once you get a few masts to climax the rest will jump in and get their jollies.

Here are safer, and even more effective, ways to prompt heat release:

- Soak a washcloth in hot water (or nuke wet in the microwave) and lay it over the rash. Make this magnificently effective by soaking the cloth in apple cider vinegar or herb tinctures listed in Stage 2 or 3 of the Remedies section. Or coat the skin first with an herbal spray.
- Warm with a heating pad or bag. Those with a moist-heat option work best. Add effectiveness by incorporating herbs.
- Hold the rash close to a heat lamp or incandescent bulb, or next to metal that's been outside in the sunlight. Best heat release I ever had was on an elbow rash using a black car in a Texas summer. Entertained a lot of people in the nearby offices that day.

Extreme Cold

Cold can also coax cells in the dermis to release their histamine, with the added benefit of cooling the rash and constricting the skin, which adds to the relief. Avoiding skin damage and infection is easier with cold.

- Start with lukewater water and stick afflicted part in the flow. Keep reducing the hot water until the flow is as cold as you can tolerate. Stand outside the shower or tub if possible.
- Apply an ice cube to the rash or through a thin cloth. Add effectiveness by making ice cubes from aloe vera, hydrosols, or watered-down herbal tinctures in Stages 1 and 2.
- Artificial ice blocks or freezer cold packs for sore muscles also work.
- Open the freezer and stick your rash-ridden body part in for a few minutes.
- Hold the rash in front of a blowing air-conditioner set in the 60-degree range or colder. Easy to do in a car.

Acids and Alkalines

The pH scale ranges from a very acidic 1.0 to a very alkaline 11.

Acids
- regular vinegar 2.8, orange juice 3.0, black coffee 5.0.

Neutrals
- milk 6.8, pure water 7.0, blood 7.4.

Alkalines
- seawater 8.0, baking soda 9.0A moderately strong acid (low pH) or alkaline (high pH)

applied to the PI rash can sometimes bring temporary relief from itching. Perhaps it acts as a counterirritant to overwhelm the nerves. For the skin, stay in the moderate 3 to 5 and 8 to 9 pH ranges. Moderately alkaline products have the added benefit of being soothing to the skin.

The thin, protective film on the outer skin is called the acid mantle. It ranges from 4.5 to 5.5 pH. If too acidic or alkaline, its beneficial bacteria can't function, and if too alkaline is more susceptible to infections. Bring the acid mantle back to its natural pH by rinsing afterward and not using skin products for a few hours to allow the natural skin oils and flora to restore. Learn more about the skin in the Rash Mastery section.

Do not use acids or alkalines if lesions or blisters are open. Strong acids and strong alkalines such as undiluted ammonia and bleach can do serious, possibly permanent, damage to your skin. More about how to remedy that in Stage 4.

Items listed are not endorsements, but used only to demonstrate the types of products available.

Alkalines

Milk of Magnesia
- Absolutely heavenly application of magnesium. Look for those without added sweetener, aspirin or antacid. The mint-flavored version aids with cooling. Or add a few drops of essential oils from Stage 2 to the regular version. Keep a bottle in the refrigerator and daub it on with cotton balls. Slather it on and wrap with gauze for overnight relief (and messy sheets).

Baking Soda
- Mix baking soda with enough water — or better yet, real witch hazel astringent — to create a poultice and slather it on. Or blend into a gauze compress. Add essential oils or tinctures from Stage 2 for more rash relief. Ground up Alka-Seltzer Gold (the aspirin-free version) will do in a pinch. Or make a concentrated Alka-Seltzer solution and dribble it on; bubbles provide a light scratch. Use only if lesions and blisters are not open.

Vegetables and fruits
- On the alkaline end are avocado, asparagus, broccoli, Brussels sprouts, garbanzo beans, honeydew melon, lima bean, mushroom, olive (non-fermented), soybean, spinach, summer squash, and tofu.

Bleach
- Use no stronger than a 10% solution. Add ¼ cup to 2 ½ to 3 cups of water.

Ammonia
- Use no stronger than a 10% solution. Add ¼ cup to 2 ½ to 3 cups of water.

Acids

Vinegar
- Apple cider vinegar works the best and hurts the least. Rice vinegar is next preferable. Most vinegar is too acidic for non-masochists.

Buttermilk
- If you can find it. Or add a tablespoon of lemon juice to a cup of milk or a couple teaspoons of lemon juice to a quarter-cup of half-and-half or cream. It's just as decadently soothing as it sounds.

Coffee
- Strong, black.

Vegetables
- Tomato packs an acidic punch, but corn, rhubarb, spinach, winter squash, and many types of pea and bean are lightly acidic, as well as any fermented or cured vegetable.

Fruits
- Fruits tend toward acidic, but citrus such as lemon, lime, and orange are the most. Blueberry, cranberry, currant, grape, pineapple,

pomegranate, strawberry and sour varieties of fruits such as sour apple also rank.

Vitamin C
- Much of fruit acidity comes from ascorbic acid, also called vitamin C. There are several lines of facial care products with generous amounts of vitamin C.

Counter-irritants

Most home remedies are counter-irritants. It's the bright shiny object technique, giving the brain something to focus on other than the itch. People get desperate and are willing to try anything on the rash. Usually it's overkill, something horrid like white shoe polish or WD-40, akin to cleaning a bathtub with a blowtorch. For the crazy things people try, and why they work or don't, visit the PI Reader section.

Substances that are too harsh cause skin damage. That lengthens the rash and causes the itch to come roaring back meaner than ever. Why not use strong herbs that provide a counter-irritant effect while also getting at the roots of itch by taming inflammation or cooling the rash? Discover all those herbs in Stages 2 and 3 of the Rash Remedies section.

Food Enzymes

Enzymes are active and that activity can provide a gentle scratch. Most meat tenderizers contain bromelain, an enzyme extracted from pineapples, but often include salt, sugar, and cornstarch — not great for skin wounds. Bromelain is also part of most digestive enzyme blends, along with papain from papayas.

Or go straight to the source by applying fruit directly. Fruits with high enzyme content like papaya and pineapples are useful, and watermelon and other melon rinds are worth a try. Fruits that oxidize and turn brown easily are also a good choice: apples, avocados, bananas, mushrooms, peaches, pears, and potatoes.

Meat Tenderizer, Unseasoned by McCormick
- Without salt, sugar or cornstarch. Mix a ¼ teaspoon of tenderizer with 1 teaspoon of water to make a paste.

Omega-Zyme - Digestive Enzyme Blend by Garden of Life
- Bromelain, papain, and much more. Slather on skin for itch, ingest for better health. Mix a ¼ teaspoon of enzymes with 1 teaspoon of water to make a paste.

Night Gloves

A sad fact is that we scratch in our sleep. A lot. And with fingernails! Can't fool the itch when you're unconscious. Cheap washable white-cotton beauty gloves are your friends. Even you manly men. Folks super-moisturize their hands at night and cover with these. Eczema patients also depend on them. Available at beauty stores. But any soft cloth gloves will do. If you yank them off in your sleep, use rubber bands on the cuffs.

For information on PI in the news and updates on products, please visit the book website:

WWW.ITCHY.BIZ

Section 4 / Chapter 2

The Stages: Your Key To Rash Relief

Chapter Index
- Stage 1: Interrupt the Rash
- Stage 2: Master the Itch
- Stage 3: Manage the Blisters
- Stage 4: Heal the Skin

The rash of poison oak and ivy (abbreviated in *Itchy Business* as PI) goes through three stages, with a fourth skin-healing phase that follows. Each stage demands unique care approaches. One product does not fit all. Because smaller and lighter exposures to PI take longer to manifest than heavier ones, once a bit of rash appears it's quite likely there's more to come. Often all stages are going at once, complicating treatment.

For more on the PI rash process, see the Rash Mastery section. Products and practices for rash relief are in the next section, Rash Remedies.

Stage 1: Stop the Rash Before it Starts

DAY 1 TO 3 (after exposure)

A mob of T-cells is brewing. The immune system mood is bad, paranoid, twitchy. As immune cells grab urushiol [oo-roo-**shee**-ohl] and drag it into the dermis, rumors about it are spreading, growing more grandiose.

The Rash: The rash begins to manifest in inflammation, redness and swelling, a slightly bumpy texture caused by emerging papules, a flushed feeling of heat, and possible tinges of itch.

First Aid: Now you know the general location of your PI exposure. Swiftly interrupt the rash with creams containing steroids, oxygen, or certain herbs.

Action: You can also try solvents and special scrubs to remove the urushiol though these limit your treatment options.

> The abbreviation "PI" refers to both poison oak and poison ivy.

Stage 2: Manage the Itch

DAY 3 TO 6

Urushiol is deep in the dermis. The immune system goes berserk and calls in the killer T-cells that blast the alien invader and everything near it. Mob mentality rules and inflammatory mediators excite the riot.

The Rash: Rash breakouts identify the place of urushiol contact, often in a line or patch where the leaf or stem brushed the skin. Papules (bumps) erupt into pinhead-sized vesicles (mini blisters) that swell into larger bullae. Lesions appear as if corrosive chemicals bubbled up from below. Capillaries become congested with immune cells and sometimes burst, causing redness and tender skin. Everything swells up. Widespread agitation shows as a serious itch that becomes unbearable.

First Aid: Now the focus is keeping the vesicles and bullae from blooming into bigger blisters. Do that by reducing inflammation through the Cs: calm, cool, and constrict. Overusing heat and rash products make infection in this stage a real possibility.

Stage 3: Manage the Blisters

DAY 6 TO 10

Skin bubbles up like asphalt on a hot day. The immune-system riot in the skin builds and peaks.

The Rash: Bullae become blisters, spilling fluid that forms an uncomfortable crust. Damaged blood vessels allow plasma in the blood to leech out (gross!), causing the area to swell with painful edema. The nervy itch builds in excruciating waves that peak, subside, and build up again.

First Aid: The skin is too raw and gummy for many of the calming and cooling potions. The focus now is on constricting the swelling, drying the blisters, softening the crust, and distracting the itch. Scratching blisters, especially during sleep, invites infection.

Stage 4: Heal the Skin

DAY 10 TO 14

The T-cell mob goes back to the immune system, leaving behind a stewing mess of cellular detritus, none of it in a good mood. Rebuilding begins and cells get busy forming new skin, layer by microscopic layer.

The Rash: Blisters peel, exposing raw, tender skin. Dry and dying skin cells are itchy business. Strafed skin cries out for fluids.

First Aid: Attention is needed to prevent scarring. Tender dry needs protection and moisturizing. Skin-care products can encourage the growth of new cells.

PLEASE READ THESE CAUTIONS

Do you feel sick from the rash? You may need immediate medical attention. Read the chapter When To See a Doctor — Fast! in the Rash Mastery section.

If there are open cuts or lesions, broken skin or blisters, or otherwise abraded skin, be extra cautious with topical products.

Read labels carefully for contraindications.

Always consult with a physician first if you are pregnant or nursing, on medications or supplements, or have an acute or chronic health condition.

All topical products can cause contact dermatitis. If skin becomes additionally dry, red, inflamed or itchy, stop using the product.

If you have sensitive skin, test prior to use by applying to a small area first and monitoring for skin reactions.

Section 4 / Chapter 3

The Cs of Itch Relief

Chapter Index
- Calm: Soothers
- Cool: Aromatics
- Constrict: Astringents

In the Rash Mastery section you heard about a variety of mental Control techniques to master the rash of poison oak and ivy (abbreviated in *Itchy Business* as PI). Earlier in this section you learned how to Confuse the itch. Now meet the rest of the Cs: Calm the inflammation, Cool the rash reactivity, and Constrict the swelling and blisters.

Remember: Be a PI ninja. Focus. Work smarter, not harder. Treat each C separately, rather than expecting one product to cover all bases, usually badly. For instance, begin the day with constricting potions, focus on cooling in the afternoon, and settle in with calming techniques at night. But you may find that calming the rash before work helps the day go better.

Calm: Soothers

PI is an angry rash. Soothe the little psycho by reducing inflammation. A calmer rash is less itchy rash and less likely to get infected. Everybody chill. Just say no to blisters. Soak in a warm mineral bath. Really, it helps.

Minerals like zinc oxide, magnesium and fine clays, and luscious goos such as aloe vera and oatmeal, are rash stand-bys. New techniques include high-oxygen creams featuring silver. Even good old oatmeal has gotten high-tech these days.

But the stars of this sprawling category are the anti-inflammatory herbs, many available in easy to use sprays and potent tinctures that can be used to make poultices, sprays, and turn conventional products into PI potions. You won't believe how strong a modest little plant like grindelia is against rashes.

Cool: Aromatics

The PI rash entails severe skin inflammation and inflammation equals heat. Cool water and gentle breezes chill through evaporation. So do aromatic analgesics like menthol and natural camphor. The intense cooling sensation as they evaporate can be a very effective counter-irritant and reduces rash swelling as well. And if your rash is too tender to touch, there are sprays and even cooling powders.

Constrict: Astringents

Blisters are awful, swollen, and messy. Help contain the blisters by constricting or shrinking blood vessels and pores with astringents like witch hazel, salicylic acid, aluminum, and tannin from black tea. Astringents reduce the heat of the PI rash, which aids with the itch.

For information on PI in the news and updates on products, please visit the book website:

WWW.ITCHY.BIZ

Section 4 / Chapter 4

Plants and Minerals for Rash

Chapter Index
- Plant Glossary
- Mineral Glossary
- From Potions to Lotions: How to Apply Them

Get to know your herbal allies. Sweet rash relief lies ahead. Exciting research on plants and minerals for skin rashes has unlocked their potential for poison oak and ivy (abbreviated in *Itchy Business* as PI). This section gives fascinating and helpful details on them, plus how to apply. Specific products and techniques reside in the Rash Remedies section.

Plants Glossary

Details on herbs come from top-flight sources like the American Botanical Association and National Library of Medicine PubMed databases. Specific citations are in the Bibliography. Even with such in-depth research, herbs are variable and effect people individually. Quality of the herb and herbal product greatly impacts effectiveness.

Aloe vera (*Aloe barbadensis*)

A succulent with long thick leaves used on the skin for over 6000 years. The interior mucilaginous gel is ultra soothing with a strong record in

Aloe Vera

treating itchy rashes and burns. Emphasis on strong. Studies indicate it downregulates inflammatory cytokine production, interferes with the production of pro-inflammatory prostaglandins, and promotes circulation to rash areas. Wonderful as a base for herbs, excellent mixed into a warm bath. Freeze into ice cubes and discover rash bliss. Use 100% aloe vera gel. Safe for children. Anti-inflammatory.
- Stage 2: Master the Itch — Calming
- Stage 4: Heal the Skin

Borage (*Borago officinalis*)

European herb treasured for its delicate blue flowers and cucumber aroma of its leaves. Most effective as a

Borage

high gamma-linolenic acid (GLA) essential oil that soothes distressed skin. Has a delicate scent. Anti-inflammatory.
- Stage 2: Master the Itch — Calming
- Stage 4: Repair the Skin

Burdock, also known as gobo (*Arctium lappa*)

A large-leafed herb favored in traditional Chinese medicine for skin. Its root is a staple of many sushi rolls. Said to have a tonifying effect on blood vessels. Contains inulin that helps against bacterial

Burdock

infection. Anti-inflammatory, antiseptic.
- Stage 4: Repair the Skin

Calendula (*Calendula officinalis*)

Soothing yet potent daisy-like annual with medium yellow flowers. Long-time popular herb for skin, widely used on babies, yet very powerful. Calendula sprays

Calendula

are proof that God loves us. Increases formation of collagen and new tissue at rash sites. Anti-allergic, anti-inflammatory, antiseptic.
- Stage 1: Interrupt the Rash
- Stage 2: Master the Itch — Calming
- Stage 4: Heal the Skin

Camphor (*Cinnamomum camphora*)

Camphor

Sharply pungent extract of camphor laurel, a large resinous evergreen tree that flourishes in Southeast Asia, and also from the kapur tree (Dryobalanops aromatic). Some species of rosemary when dried contain up to 20% camphor. But most camphor on drugstore shelf products is synthetically produced from oil of turpentine. In 1980, the U.S. Food and Drug Administration capped products at 11% synthetic camphor, outright banned several versions, and generally discourages the synthetic's use.
- Stage 3: Master the Itch — Cooling

Chamomile, German (*Matricaria recutita*)

Chamomile, German

The quintessential calming herb is a delicate daisy-like flower. Easy to come by as herbal tea bags, but the essential oil is more effective on skin. Its anti-inflammatory flavones penetrate surprisingly deep into the dermis. Blue chamomile is a famed skin oil made from chamomile plants bred for a high azulene content, found as bisabolol or matricaria in superior beauty products for sensitive skin. Safe for children. Anti-allergic, anti-inflammatory, antimicrobial.
- Stage 2: Master the Itch — Calming
- Stage 4: Heal the Skin

> Items listed are not endorsements, but used only to demonstrate the types of products available.

Cilantro/coriander (*Coriandrum sativum*)

Cilantro

Cilantro is a common green herb in Mexican and other cuisines. Its seeds, called coriander, provide a warm spice popular in European, Middle Eastern, and Indian cooking. Thought in Ayurvedic medicine to be very cooling. The leaves are considered effective in draining retained fluids. Anti-inflammatory, antimicrobial, antioxidant.
- Stage 2: Master the Itch — Cooling
- Stage 3: Manage the Blisters — Constricting

Coleus, Indian (*Coleus forskohlii*)

Coleus

India cousin of the common houseplant with a camphor-like aroma. Source of cholesterol drug Forskolin. Super effective at halting the rash in the early stages because its acetylcholinesterase inhibition desensitizes mast cells, the source of histamine. Patients with bleeding disorders or low blood pressure should not use this herb. Anti-inflammatory.
- Stage 1: Interrupt the Rash

Comfrey (*Symphytum officinale*)

Comfrey

Large-leafed herb with a large mucilaginous root; both parts are use in herbal medicine. The base ingredient for most "green salves," it is most associated with bone healing, but considered soothing for skin because of its high allantoin content. Not to be used on open wounds or broken blisters. Anti-inflammatory.
- Stage 1: Interrupt the Rash
- Stage 2: Master the Itch — Calming

Echinacea, also called coneflower *(Echinacea purpurea)*

Echinacea

Considered a potent herb for stimulating the immune system and inhibiting infection. Other species such as Echinacea pallida suppress immune response and might be more effective on the PI rash but are not commonly available. Anti-allergic, anti-inflammatory, antiseptic, astringent.
- Stage 1: Interrupt the Rash
- Stage 2: Master the Itch — Calming
- Stage 3: Manage the Blisters — Constricting

Eucalyptus, blue gum *(Eucalyptus globulus)*

Eucalyptus, blue gum

A tropical tree with a strong, resinous scent that flourishes in Australia. Antibacterial.
- Stage 2: Master the Itch — Cooling
- Stage 3: Manage the Blisters — Constricting

Evening primrose *(Oenothera biennis)*

Evening Primrose

Native yellow wildflower whose seeds are pressed to make a high gamma-linolenic acid (GLA) essential oil. Soothes distressed skin and reduces swelling. Some essential fatty acid supplements contain the oil. Has a light scent. Anti-inflammatory.
- Stage 3: Manage the Blisters — Constricting
- Stage 4: Repair the Skin

Goldenseal *(Hydrastis canadensis)*

Goldenseal

Considered a potent herb for stimulating the immune system and soothing mucous membranes. Contains berberine, considered in Traditional Chinese Medicine to drain the damp heat of a rash. Conflicts with some prescription drugs, use with caution. Anti-inflammatory, antimicrobial.
- Stage 1: Interrupt the Rash
- Stage 2: Master the Itch — Calming

Grindelia, also called gumweed *(Grindelia robusta, Grindelia camporum)*

Grindelia

Grindelia is a low scrub bush with sharp resinous scent native to California and Baja California. The plant is sticky and buds of the bright yellow flowers fill with a white gum. Has tested well at specifically combating the PI rash, so effective that it's featured in drugstore products. Revered by Native Americans for its PI rash relief and respiratory soothing powers. Superb at PI rash prevention. Anti-inflammatory.
- Stage 1: Interrupt the Rash
- Stage 2: Master the Itch — Calming

Helichrysum *(Helichrysum italicum)*

Helichrysum

Mediterranean plant known for its bright and dryable yellow flowers. Most effective as an essential oil that soothes distressed skin. Has an unusual herbal, woody, somewhat camphorous, scent. Anti-inflammatory, antiseptic.
- Stage 1: Interrupt the Rash
- Stage 2: Master the Itch — Calming
- Stage 4: Repair the Skin

Horse chestnut *(Aesculus hippocastanum)*

Horse Chestnut

Seeds of the river-loving tree have long used to hasten healing from bruises, varicose veins, hemorrhoids, and even chronic venous insufficiency with its

tonifying effect on blood vessels. Horse chestnut is also taken internally to improve microcirculation and strengthen vein walls. Anti-inflammatory.
- Stage 4: Repair the Skin

Jewelweed, orange *(Impatiens capensis)*

The herbal pop star in the PI rash arena is jewelweed, a naturalized variety of impatiens with orange orchid-like flowers. The stems are succulent and the dull leaf surface takes on a jeweled look when submersed in water. Found in moist shady areas with high humus soil, especially wooded bottomlands where it tolerates flooding. Big anecdotal reputation as a PI rash treatment, but performs poorly in tests. However, it's undeniably a great soother. It seems to work best when the thick juice is squeezed from the succulent stems and applied to the rash. If you're lucky, you can collect some, squeeze it, and preserve the juice as ice cubes. Anti-inflammatory.

Jewelweed

- Stage 1: Interrupt the Rash
- Stage 2: Master the Itch— Calming

Lavender, true, also called common, English or narrow-leaved *(Lavandula angustifolia)*

Long esteemed for its enchanting aroma that brings about relaxation in all but the biggest brutes. It excels as an essential oil and is especially great in baths. Topically applied has been proven to reduce scarring. Lavender hydrosols are heaven to the skin. Lavandin hybrids are considered not as effective. Lavender essential oil is all too commonly faked with synthetic aromas, so purchase astutely. Anti-inflammatory, antimicrobial, antispasmodic.

Lavender, true

- Stage 2: Master the Itch — Calming
- Stage 4: Heal the Skin

Mint, including peppermint *(Mentha piperita)* and spearmint *(Mentha spicata)*

Renowned for its brisk cooling effects. Menthol can be refined from plants or created synthetically.

Mint

- Stage 2: Master the Itch — Cooling

Oats *(Avena sativa)*

A long-time remedy for irritated skin. Pulverized oatmeal is superb as a bath and leaves a light protective coating on the skin. An extract of green oats is a stronger nervine for soothing nerve tips and excels as a compress. Aveno has the science of oatmeal down, especially in their Active Naturals line. Their lotions with colloidal oatmeal provide both moisture and a protective barrier for the skin. They even use oat oil! Who knew there was such a thing? Anti-inflammatory.

Oats

- Stage 2: Master the Itch — Calming
- Stage 4: Heal the Skin

Plantain, also called ribwort *(Plantago lanceolata)*

Plantain is related to psyllium of Metamucil fame, and the whole plant is high in mucopolysaccharides. Soothes like a mix of aloe and honey, and is wonderful as a base for herbs. Also seems to have immunostimulatory qualities. Anti-inflammatory.

Plantain

- Stage 1: Interrupt the Rash
- Stage 2: Master the Itch — Calming

For information on PI in the news and updates on products, please visit the book website:

WWW.ITCHY.BIZ

Rose hip (*Rosa moschata*, also *Rosa canina* and *Rosa rubiginosa*)

Seeds of the wild rose provide a high gamma-linolenic acid (GLA) oil that increases skin flexibility and reduces scars. Anti-inflammatory.

Rose hips

- Stage 2: Master the Itch — Calming
- Stage 4: Heal the Skin

Rosemary (*Rosmarinus officinalis*)

European woody herb with narrow oily leaves and a strong resinous scent. Anti-inflammatory, antiseptic.

Rosemary

- Stage 2: Master the Itch — Cooling

Sassafras (*Sassafras officinale*)

Essential to Louisiana Creole cuisine, the fragrant tree grows in moist areas of the eastern U.S. Slightly numbing to the skin. Analgesic, antiseptic.

Sassafras

- Stage 2: Master the Itch — Cooling
- Stage 3: Manage the Blisters

Tea, black (*Camellia sinensis*)

Black teas are high in tannins, a superb astringent, and those in cloth tea bags are handy as poultices. Use water at a hard boil and steep for several minutes. British breakfast and other strong teas have the most tannin. Astringent.

Tea, black

- Stage 3: Manage Blisters — Constricting

Tea tree (*Melaleuca alternifolia*)

Oily tree native to Australia. Usually sold as an oil but tinctures are available. Low cineole oils are easier on the skin. Tea tree oil can be sub par and even purposefully oxidized, so purchase carefully. Antimicrobial.

Tea tree

- Stage 2: Master the Itch — Constricting
- Stage 3: Manage the Blisters

Turmeric (*Curcuma longa*)

High curcumin content. Seldom used topically since it dyes skin orange. Mixing with topical clays abates that a great deal. Anti-inflammatory, antiseptic.

Turmeric

- Stage 2: Master the Itch — Calming
- Stage 3: Manage the Blisters

White oak (*Quercus alba*)

Classic shade tree whose inner bark is high in tannins, yet very soothing. Anti-allergic, antibacterial, anti-inflammatory, astringent.

White oak

- Stage 2: Master the Itch — Calming
- Stage 3: Manage the Blisters

Witch hazel (*Hamamelis virginiana*)

A small tree whose tannin-rich wood is long revered for its gentle yet effective astringent quality and ability to reduce swelling and redness. It strengthens the surface proteins of skin cells, forming a protective layer, and accelerates healing. Look

Witch hazel

for versions without added isopropyl alcohol. Witch hazel is plenty powerful on its own. Anti-inflammatory, astringent.
- Stage 2: Master the Itch — Constricting
- Stage 3: Manage the Blisters

> Items listed are not endorsements, but used only to demonstrate the types of products available.

Mineral Glossary

Aluminum

Valued for its drying quality, making it a staple in antiperspirants and the basis of Domeboro, a version of Burow's solution. The soft, silvery, non-ferrous metal is pervasive on the planet, the most abundant metal in the Earth's crust, yet it is not metabolized by the human body, causing toxicity problems with extensive use. Astringent.
- Stage 3: Manage the Blisters

Kaolin, also called china clay

Soft, pale, fine-textured phyllosilicate clay, sometimes found mixed with iron oxide to give it a pink hue. Sets up an alkaline environment on the skin, calms the rash and absorbs blister fluid. A key ingredient in Kaopectate and calamine, the clay can be bought separately and mixed with herbal tinctures to make custom coatings.
- Stage 2: Master the Itch
- Stage 3: Manage the Blisters

Magnesium

Many forms are highly alkaline. Found in most bath soaks, it relaxes mind and muscles. Magnesium sulfate is Epsom salts. Magnesium hydroxide is the key ingredient in Milk of Magnesia.
- Stage 2: Master the Itch
- Stage 3: Manage the Blisters

Sodium

The sixth most common element in the Earth's crust, it is essential to plant and animal life. One of the alkali metals, it dissolves easily in water and contributes to the neutral pH of the ocean.
- Stage 2: Master the Itch
- Stage 3: Manage the Blisters

Sulfur

An abundant element with a rotten-egg aroma, it has a keratolytic effect that removes dead skin cells, helping new ones to grow. De-odorized 10% sulfur creams are marketed to help with acne, scabies, rosacea and cracked skin. Antibacterial, anti-demodectic, antifungal.
- Stage 4: Heal the Skin

Zinc oxide

A white mineral powder that soothes skin. Insoluble quality makes it popular in diaper rash creams and sunscreens. Calamine lotion contains zinc oxide and (pink) ferric oxide. Antibacterial, antiseptic.
- Stage 2: Master the Itch

From Potions to Lotions: How to Apply

Step beyond the usual drugstore creams to discover more effective ways of applying healing compounds to the skin for the rash of poison oak and ivy (abbreviated in Itchy Business as PI).

Compresses

Cotton squares or gauze pads are saturated with hydrosols, astringents, diluted tinctures, or other liquids and placed upon the skin. Sometimes rash locations enable holding the compress in place by medical tape or stretch wrap. Pre-moistened towelettes can also be used.

Essential Oils

Essential oils are volatile aromatic compounds distilled from plants. Used correctly, they can have amazing effects on the skin. Remember to breathe in the essential oils for best effect. Keep essential oils away from eyes and mucous membranes. Follow product directions carefully. Available online and at natural food stores. Quality lines of essential oils include Aromaceuticals, Mountain Rose, Native American Nutritionals, and Plant Therapy.

Essential Oils bottle

Do not apply essential oils directly to skin unless diluted.

- Blend a few drops with a ¼ cup of plant, nut or seed oil or a light base such as aloe vera or glycerin, to create a cream or lotion.
- Dilute a few drops in ½ cup water, witch hazel, isopropyl (rubbing) or ethyl (drinking) alcohol to use as a spray or soak a compress.
- Mix several drops into a paste of ¼ cup each bentonite clay and water, and thin with a base lotion, to create a calamine-type product.

Hydrosols

Also called hydrolats and distillate waters, it's the lightly fragrant fluid that remains after steam distillation of essential oils. Chill hydrosols in the refrigerator for extra cooling effect. They can be daubed on the rash, applied as a wet compress, used as a spray, or frozen into ice cubes. Hydrosols are always gentle. Available online and at natural food stores. Quality lines of hydrosols include Aromaceuticals, Mountain Rose, Native American Nutritionals, and Plant Therapy.

Lotions and Creams

A lotion or cream may not be as potent as tinctures or sprays, but will keep the herbs on your skin for a longer period. Most brands contain a token amount. Increase potency by adding essential oils or tinctures. Avoid lotions with greasy, lanolin or petroleum jelly or mineral oil bases. PI rash heals better when air can circulate freely. Quality lines of lotions and creams include Boericke & Tafel, Herb Pharm, and Weleda.

Poultices

The simplest form of herb application: moisten, mash, and slather plant material on skin. Sometimes rash locations are in areas that allow the poultice to be covered by gauze and held in place by medical tape or stretch wrap. Easiest are herbal tea bags: Drink the tea; apply the bag.

Bulk herbs, herbal teas, and clay are available online and at natural food stores. Limited types of herb teas are available at most grocery stores. Quality lines of bulk herbs include Frontier, Mountain Rose, and Starwest Botanicals. Quality lines of teas include Celestial Seasonings, Choice Teas, Davidson's, Frontier Herbs, Mighty Leaf, Mountain Rose, Republic of Tea, Starwest Botanicals, and Traditional Medicinals.

PLEASE READ THESE CAUTIONS

Do you feel sick from the rash? You may need immediate medical attention. Read the chapter When To See a Doctor — Fast! in the Rash Mastery section.

If there are open cuts or lesions, broken skin or blisters, or otherwise abraded skin, be extra cautious with topical products.

Read labels carefully for contraindications.

Always consult with a physician first if you are pregnant or nursing, on medications or supplements, or have an acute or chronic health condition.

All topical products can cause contact dermatitis. If skin becomes additionally dry, red, inflamed or itchy, stop using the product.

If you have sensitive skin, test prior to use by applying to a small area first and monitoring for skin reactions.

Sprays

Sprays are basically tinctures, extracts and sometimes essential oils diluted with water or isopropoyl (rubbing) or cetyl (drinking) alcohol. Super easy to make your own. Hydrosols are ready made to be sprays. Use a small travel cosmetic spray bottle. Great for rash patches that sprawl. Quality lines of sprays include Gaia Herbs, Herb Pharm, and Weleda. Chill sprays in the refrigerator for extra cooling. Remember to breathe in the aroma for best effect.

Tinctures

Tinctures are concentrated alcohol- and glycerite-based herbal extracts that come in tiny bottles with dropper tops. Readily absorbed into the skin, a few can be daubed directly on the rash, but most are diluted for topical use. Tinctures in glycerite can be just the thing on tender skin and blend well with lotions. Those based on alcohol make excellent sprays to help dry up the rash. Remember to breathe the aroma in as well for best effect.

Blend several drops with ¼ cup of plant, nut, or seed oil, or a light base such as aloe vera or glycerin, to create a cream or lotion.
- Aloe based-blends can freeze into ice cubes.

Dilute 1 teaspoon in ½ cup water, witch hazel, isopropyl (rubbing) or ethyl (drinking) alcohol to use as a spray or soak a compress.
- Saturate a washcloth, heat in the microwave, and apply for a healing safe scratch.
- If using a non-alcohol solution, freeze to create ice cubes.

Mix several drops into a paste of ¼ cup each bentonite clay and water, and thin with a base lotion, to create a calamine-type product.

Available online and at natural food stores. Quality lines of tinctures and extracts include Mountain Rose, Gaia Herbs, and Herb Pharm.

5

Rash Remedies: Minimize the Misery

Section Index

1. Stage 1 – Interrupting the Rash
2. Stage 2 – Calming the Rash
3. Stage 2 – Cooling the Itch
4. Stage 3 – Constricting the Blisters
5. Stages 2 and 3 – Analgesics for Pain Relief
6. Stage 4 – Renewing the Skin
7. Holistic: Treat the Body, Reduce the Rash

This mega-section demystifies the usual potions for the rash of poison oak and ivy (abbreviated in Itchy Business as PI). There are terrific new options out there, especially in the holistic realm. You'll be amazed at the power of a little plant called grindelia, which is especially effective on PI, and the yellow daisy calendula, capable of taming bad rashes, even epic baby-butt.

A few products in this section aren't even marketed for treating PI — Milk of Magnesia, for instance — and a really rockin' feminine itch cream. (Come on guys, you can do it!) You'll learn how to easily create inexpensive yet highly effective PI remedies from common household products, plus how to modify your own skin products with herbal tinctures and essential oils. Better yet, you'll understand why they work.

Section 5 / Chapter 1

Stage 1 – Interrupting the Rash

Chapter Index
- Topical Steroids
- Topical Herbs
- Oxygen Creams
- Homeopathics
- Oral Antihistamines

After potential exposure to PI, stay extremely observant, but not paranoid, to changes in your skin: a bit of heat, a bumpy or mottled texture, some swelling, the inklings of an itch. Sometimes you can stop the rash in its tracks by subduing or confusing the immune response.

Because lighter touches of PI take longer to arise as a rash, often the first small appearance signals a larger rash to come. It's worth a chance at this time to give the solvent and oxygen water cleaning methods detailed in the Understanding Urushiol section one last try.

> Practice safe scratch! Learn how in the Your Rash Toolkit section.

Topical Steroids

Applied before the rash ramps up, non-prescription corticosteroid creams such as 1% hydrocortisone can sometimes interrupt the T-cell mediated immune response. Their power to halt the rash at this stage can be amazing. It is an option for rash areas that have been cleaned only with water or detergent, not with alcohol, oxygen or solvents.

Look for versions of corticosteroid creams that come in non-greasy aloe vera or oatmeal bases. Do not use cooling versions with added menthol; let the focus be on steroid's immune system powers. Repeat as often as the label allows but no further. Stop if the rash arises.

> The abbreviation "PI" refers to both poison oak and poison ivy.

Corticosteroids are super powerful drugs. Used daily for long periods, topical versions can cause irreversible thinning of the skin, making it much more sensitive to sunlight and irritants. Can you say "permanent skin damage"?

Lotions And Creams

1% Hydrocortisone Anti-Itch Cream by Aveeno
- Mellowed out with oatmeal.

Cortizone 10 Maximum Strength Feminine Itch Cream by Chattem
- Softened with aloe, suitable for all types of skin.

Topical Herbs

Super anti-inflammatory or anti-allergy herbs applied topically can nip a PI rash in the bud for some people. Perhaps it inhibits the skin's immune system. Or maybe it just confuses the rash reaction so much it loses momentum.

Herbs considered to be anti-allergy and anti-inflammation include:

- Echinacea, also called coneflower (*Echinacea purpurea*)
- Goldenseal (*Hydrastis canadensis*)
- Grindelia, also called gumweed (*Grindelia robusta*)
- Indian coleus (*Coleus forskolli*)
- Plantain, also called plantago (*Plantago lanceolata*)

Tinctures

Tinctures are alcohol or glycerin-based herbal solutions in small bottles with dropper tops. Blend several drops with ¼ cup of plant, nut or seed oil or a light base such as aloe vera or glycerin. Remember to breathe the aroma in as well for best effect.

Coleus Forskohlii Root by Gaia Herbs.
- Powerful stuff for rash interupt! Use sparingly.

Sprays

Great for rash patches that sprawl. Make your own sprays by blending alcohol tinctures with water, witch hazel, or isopropyl (rubbing) alcohol or ethyl (drinking) alcohol; directions under Tinctures. Remember to breathe in the aroma for best effect.

Be Gone Scratch-N-Itch by Washington Homeopathics
- A whopping amount of grindelia (17%) plus natural camphor in an ethyl (drinking) alcohol base. Brisk! Does not leave a protective film on skin, which some prefer.

Rash Relief Spray by Tecnu
- Calendula, grindelia, and plantain in a glycerine and ethyl (drinking) alcohol base. Available at most drugstores. Also contains astringent green tea extract, antiseptic tea tree and white thyme oils, and cooling menthol. Amazing product. Moderates skin reactions of many kinds. Leaves a slight protective film on the skin. Grindelia's sharp, resinous aroma is the smell of relief. Do not confuse with the most famous Tecnu product, its Outdoor Skin Cleanser, which should not be used once the rash erupts.

Soothing Oak & Ivy by Herb Pharm
- A potent and aromatic combination of grindelia, sassafras, and natural menthol in an ethyl (drinking) alcohol base moderated by glycerin. Superbly cooling. Leaves a surface film that is very protective

---

For information on PI in the news and updates on products, please visit the book website:
WWW.ITCHY.BIZ

Oxygen Creams

Being a phenolic compound, urushiol may be impacted by concentrations of oxygen. Theory is that oxygen creams might help at this stage. Rub in firmly. Do not use oxygen creams and then use a solvent such as Tecnu or a scrub like Zanfel. Do not use oxygen products in conjunction with strong acids or alkalines.

Gly-Oxide Liquid Antiseptic Oral Cleanser
- Synthetic base with 10% carbamide peroxide, a source of hydrogen peroxide.

Oxy Bump Saline Oxygen Nasal Spray by Oxy Bump
- Blast it with stabilized oxygen in a soothing base of saline and plant minerals.

Terrasil Itch, Rash & Pain Relief by Aidance Skincare
- A highly active space-age cream with oxygen-rich oxides of magnesium, silver, and zinc in a base of bentonite clay, jojoba oil and beeswax. Graced by cooling oils of eucalyptus and peppermint oil, and a touch of silver for antiseptic.

Triple Oxygen + C Energizing Cream by Bliss
- Pricey facial cream, but loaded with oxygen.

Whipped Oxygen Cream by kNutek
- Soothing jojoba oil, grape seed oil, and honey, with vitamins A and E, and a cool-sounding oxygen plasma.

Zim's Crack Crème
- No, not that crack. Hydrogen peroxide gel for cracked skin.

Homeopathics

Homeopathy is a form of medicine developed in Europe postulating that minute traces of botanicals and other substances can stimulate the body's defenses in very specific ways. Though ineffective according to most U.S. studies, some people swear by it.

The main homeopathic remedy for PI is called Rhus tox, after the old botany nomenclature, *Rhus toxicodendron*. It is an undetectable trace of urushiol in a sugar pill or potion. Theory is that it will act like a vaccine and desensitize your reactions to PI. So there may be some success in taking it before or right after exposure.

- Boericke & Tafel: **Oral Ivy**
- Hyland's: **Poison Ivy/Oak Tablets**
- KingBio Natural Medicine: **Poison Ivy/Oak Relief**
- Washington Homeopathics: **Be Gone Poison Ivy**

Oral Antihistamines

Antihistamines calm the body's allergic response, but they're not greatly effective with PI. Oral antihistamines may help some as a preventative if you are greatly sensitive or anxious about your exposure. Try taking a small daily dose until you know if a rash will arise.

Antihistamines, even short term, can have some persnickety side effects. Be sure to check for possible interactions with any medication you might be taking.

Of the over-the-counter antihistamines, diphenhydramine (**Benadryl**, etc.) is the strongest, but sleep inducing for many. If a rash ensues and the itch is horrible, that quality can be a godsend. Look for liquid children's versions that allow easy adjusting of the dose. Next in strength is chlorpheniramine maleate (**Chlor-Trimeton**, etc.), also fairly soporific. A strong antihistamine, yet non-drowsy, is cetirizine (**Zyrtec**, etc.).

> Items listed are not endorsements, but used only to demonstrate the types of products available.

PLEASE READ THESE CAUTIONS

Do you feel sick from the rash? You may need immediate medical attention. Read the chapter When To See a Doctor — Fast! in the Rash Mastery section.

If there are open cuts or lesions, broken skin or blisters, or otherwise abraded skin, be extra cautious with topical products.

Read labels carefully for contraindications.

Always consult with a physician first if you are pregnant or nursing, on medications or supplements, or have an acute or chronic health condition.

All topical products can cause contact dermatitis. If skin becomes additionally dry, red, inflamed or itchy, stop using the product.

If you have sensitive skin, test prior to use by applying to a small area first and monitoring for skin reactions.

Section 5 / Chapter 2

Stage 2 – Calming the Rash

Chapter Index
- Topical Earth
- Topical Herbs
- Water-Based Relief
- Kitchen Alkalines

Once cleaning off urushiol [oo-roo-**shee**-ohl] and Stage 1 attempts at rash interrupt are no longer effective, the rash is on. Bumpy vesicles swell with fluid, lesions appear, and the itch gets persistent. You have an adversary whether you like it or not. The most common mistake in PI rash treatment is attempting to exterminate urushiol. That's what the immune system is doing, blasting it out of existence. Your job is to minimize the damage.

Calming the rash of poison oak and ivy (abbreviated in *Itchy Business* as PI) gets at the roots of itchiness. Soothing minerals, powerful anti-inflammatory herbs, and more alleviate inflammation and distract itch. You must do everything possible to keep the vesicles of Stage 2 from swelling into bullae and blisters of Stage 3. Once that happens, your options for itch become limited — just as you need them the most. (PI is perverse.)

Topical Earth
- Clays
- Minerals

Many clays and minerals are alkalizing, soothing the savage PI rash. Keep these in the refrigerator for even more itch-relief oomph.

Clays

Calamine and Its Kin
Animals have been slathering dirt on themselves for relief since life on Earth began. Humans have become connoisseurs. Bentonite and kaolin clays are tops for their soft, absorptive alkalinity. Add some zinc oxide plus a bit of iron oxide to make it rose pink and you've got calamine. But old-fashioned calamine lotions are nearly impossible to find anymore. More often it's combined with mild numbing agents and ineffective topical antihistamines.

> The abbreviation "PI" refers to both poison oak and poison ivy.

So make your own. Cosmetic-grade bentonite clay is easy to buy online and at beauty stores. Start with one part water and one part clay, adding water until you get a soft paste. Apply that, or mix in aloe vera or glycerin to create a lotion for smoother spreading. Clay varies, so there will be some improvising. Add some drops of essential oils or tinctures recommended in Stages 3 and 4 for an amazing calamine. Add baking soda for increased alkalinity and a rather satisfying scratch when the lotion is rinsed off. This technique totally rocks.

Be sure to wash any calamine off with warm water before it dries into flakes or it'll hurt like heck when you remove it. Apply frequently for best effect.

Calamine Lotion by GSMS
- The old-fashioned kind. Enhance by adding a few drops of calming essential oils or tinctures.

Poison Ivy/Oak Spray by All Terrain
- Kaolin clay and zinc oxide in a handy spray with antiseptic neem and tea tree oils.

> Practice safe scratch! Learn how in the Your Rash Toolkit section.

Minerals

MAGNESIUM

Magnesium is mellow, super soothing and alkalizing to the skin.

Epsoma by SatisPHARMA
- Magnesium sulfate, better known as Epsom salts, in an aloe and glycerin base.

Milk of Magnesia, Original by Phillips
- Soothing application of magnesium. Look for those without added sweetener, aspirin or antacid. The mint-flavored version aids with cooling. Or add a few drops of essential oils listed above to the regular version. Instructions under Essential Oils, below. Keep a bottle in the refrigerator and daub it on with cotton balls. Slather and wrap with gauze for overnight relief (and messy sheets).

Terrasil Itch, Rash & Pain Relief by Aidance Skincare
- A highly active space-age cream with oxygen-rich oxides of magnesium, silver, and zinc in a base of bentonite clay, jojoba oil and beeswax. Graced by cooling oils of eucalyptus and peppermint oil, and a touch of silver for antiseptic.

SODIUM

Seawater is a neutral pH, which is part of why bath salts are soothing to the skin. But if you haven't time for a bath, consider a saline rinse. Make a rinse out of Epsom, Himalayan, Kosher, or sea salt, not conventional table salt.

Wound Wash by Simply Saline
- Sterile saline solution moderated with aloe vera, plus a slight numbing agent, benzalkonium chloride. Excellent on the lesions.

ZINC OXIDE

A mineral that soothes, alkalizes, and creates a protective skin barrier. Best forms are diaper rash creams since the bases tend to be non-irritating. Look for simple zinc oxide ointments, often sold as house brands at drugstores. Zinc oxide sunscreens have unneeded ingredients that don't belong on wounded skin. Avoid creams or ointments based on mineral oil or petroleum jelly.

Baby Powder by Averi Naturals
- Arrowroot and zinc oxide powders, plus calendula and lavender. Handy if skin is too tender to touch.

Rapid Relief Diaper Rash Ointment, Creamy by Desitin
- Aloe and beeswax base with 13% zinc oxide.

Soothing Relief Diaper Rash Cream by Aveeno Baby
- Base of oat extract, beeswax, and glycerin, with 13% zinc oxide and oatmeal aplenty.

Zinc Oxide Diaper Cream by Badger
- Plant oils and beeswax base with 10% zinc oxide plus oatmeal and calendula.

Topical Herbs

- Tinctures
- Sprays
- Hydrosols
- Lotions and Creams
- Botanic Oils
- Essential Oils
- Poultices

Anti-inflammatory herbs applied to the skin can be surprisingly effective in calming the PI rash and its itch. Several, such as calendula, have centuries of anecdotal history for skin health. Others, like grindelia, are effective enough to be in mainstream drugstore rash products. Some herbs also provide a counter-irritant distraction.

> Do you feel sick from the rash? You may need immediate medical attention. Read the chapter When To See a Doctor – Fast! in the Rash Mastery section.

If there are open lesions or breaking blisters, be extra careful with which herbs you apply. For instance, caution with comfrey at this stage since it's not for use on broken skin.

Tinctures

Tinctures are concentrated alcohol or glycerin-based herbal solutions in small bottles with dropper tops.

Blend several drops with ¼ cup of plant, nut, or seed oil, or a light base such as aloe vera or glycerin, to create a cream or lotion.

- *Aloe based-blends can freeze into ice cubes.*

Dilute 1 teaspoon in ½ cup water, witch hazel, isopropyl (rubbing) or ethyl (drinking) alcohol to use as a spray or soak a compress.

- *Saturate a washcloth, heat in the microwave, and apply for a healing safe scratch.*
- *If using a non-alcohol solution, freeze to create ice cubes.*

Mix several drops into a paste of ¼ cup each bentonite clay and water, and thin with a base lotion, to create a calamine-type product.

Remember to breathe in the aroma for best effect.

Cooling tinctures suitable for topical application include:

- sassafras.

Dilute in a base (directions above):

- Ultra soothing and gentle for children: calendula, chamomile, oats
- Anti-inflammatory: grindelia, plantain
- Super soother: jewelweed (orange), lavender (true)
- Blood vessel tonifier: burdock, horse chestnut

Dermal Health by HerbPharm

- Anti-inflammatory burdock, soothing sarsaparilla, and other herbs in an ethyl (drinking) alcohol and glycerin base.

Sprays

Great for rash patches that sprawl. Make your own sprays by blending alcohol tinctures with water, witch hazel, or isopropyl (rubbing) alcohol or ethyl (drinking) alcohol; directions under Tinctures. Keep chilled in the refrigerator for added cooling effect. Remember to breathe in the aroma for best effect.

Hydrosols for making into calming sprays include:

- calendula, chamomile (German), lavender.

Tinctures for diluting into calming sprays include:

- burdock, calendula, cilantro, chamomile (German), comfrey, grindelia, jewelweed (orange), lavender (true), oats (green), plantain, sassafras.

Rash Relief Spray by Tecnu

- Calendula, grindelia, and plantain in a glycerine and ethyl (drinking) alcohol base. Available at most drugstores. Also contains astringent green tea extract, antiseptic tea tree and white thyme oils, and cooling menthol. Amazing product. Moderates skin reactions of many kinds. Leaves a slight protective film on the skin. Grindelia's sharp, resinous aroma is the smell of relief. Do not confuse with the most famous Tecnu product, its Outdoor Skin Cleanser, which should not be used once the rash erupts.

Soothing Oak & Ivy by Herb Pharm

- A potent and aromatic combination of grindelia, sassafras, and natural menthol in an ethyl (drinking) alcohol base moderated by glycerin. Superbly cooling. Leaves a surface film that is very protective.

Calendula Spray by Hyland's

- Non-alcohol base and wonderfully spunky at 22% extract. Proof that God loves us.

Hydrosols

A lightly fragrant water by-product of essential oil distillation. Apply directly to skin with a dropper or dispense as a spray. Remember to breathe in the aroma in for best effect.

Chamomile Hydrosol by Mountain Rose

- Super cooling and refreshing, penetrates deeply into the skin.

Helichrysum Hydrosol by Mountain Rose
- Ultra soothing European beauty oil with an undefinable woody-herbal aroma.

Lotions and Creams

Lotions and creams are usually not as potent as tinctures or sprays, but keep the herbs on your skin longer. Make your own; directions under Tinctures and Essential Oils.

Anti-Itch Cream by Honeymark
- Manuka honey, jojoba and sunflower oil, cocoa and shea butter, colloidal oatmeal and aloe vera, infused with extracts of chamomile, comfrey, echinacea, goldenseal, and lavender, graced by allantoin and bisabolol.

Calendula products by Weleda
- A line of potent calendula lotions, creams and oils. Those for babies are extra gentle on the skin.

Califlora cream by Boericke & Tafel
- Nicely strong with calendula.

Florasonea by Boericke & Tafel
- *Cardiospermum halicacabum* can be surprisingly effective on itch.

Mountain Rose Herbal Oils
- Calming herb-infused oils include: calendula, mullein, plantain.

For information on PI in the news and updates on products, please visit the book website:

WWW.ITCHY.BIZ

Botanic Oils

As simple as it gets: oils extracted from plant seeds that are high in gamma-linolenic fatty acids (GLA). Or a carrier oil is infused with herbs. Oils, for sounding oily, absorb rapidly. Remember to breathe in the aroma for best effect.

Argan (*Argania spinosa*)
- It's a Moroccan gourmet oil, it's a cosmetic, it's argan oil, pressed from kernels of the argan tree. But use the unroasted, fast absorbing, beauty product. Argan is rich in natural vitamin E, squalene, and GLA. Use the deodorized versions or ready yourself for a trippy aroma.

Borage (*Borago officinalis*)
- Super rich in GLA. Pleasant aroma. Avoid during pregnancy.

Evening primrose (*Oenothera biennis*)
- Nicely rich in GLA. Pleasant aroma.

Mountain Rose Herbal Oils
- Calming oils for PI rash include: calendula, mullein, plantain.

Wild Rose Facial Oil
- Essential oils of helichrysum and lavender infused in a base of rosehip, jojoba, and carrot seed oils, olive oil infused with calendula flowers, and vitamin E.

Essential Oils

Powerful concentrated substances distilled from plants in small bottles with drip dispensers.

- *Blend a few drops with a ¼ cup of plant, nut or seed oil or a light base such as aloe vera or glycerin, to create a cream or lotion.*
- *Dilute a few drops in ½ cup water, witch hazel, isopropyl (rubbing) or ethyl (drinking) alcohol to use as a spray or soak a compress.*
- *Mix several drops into a paste of ¼ cup each bentonite clay and water, and thin with a base lotion, to create a calamine-type product.*

Remember to breathe the aroma in as well for best effect.

Blue chamomile (German)
- Famed blue skin oil found in superior beauty products for sensitive skin.

Helichrysum
- Ultra soothing European beauty oil with an undefinable woody-herbal aroma.

Lavender (true)
- Soothing aroma and gentle for children.

Suggested essential oil blend for skin from Aromaceuticals.com:
- 1 ounce (2 tablespoons) aloe vera gel or juice
- ¼ teaspoon calendula-infused oil
- 3 drops blue chamomile (German)
- 3 drops helichrysum
- 6 drops lavender
- 5 drops cypress

Swab onto rash several times daily. For children make it half as strong.

Poultices

Ground up plant matter moistened and slathered on skin.

Quick and easy poultice: herb tea bags. Drink the tea, apply the bag. Anti-inflammatory herbal teas include: chamomile, turmeric.

Or go with an oatmeal poultice. Soothes the skin as well as nerves, which are highly inflamed in a PI rash. Add tinctures or essential oils from Stage 2 for greater relief.

> Practice safe scratch! Learn how in the Your Rash Toolkit section.

Water–Based Relief
- Showers and Soaps
- Soaking Baths

Frequently washing with the right soaps, and occasional soaks in a tub, can greatly relieve the PI rash. Water softens crusty parts of the rash and moves dead skin cells away so new ones can arise. Rubbing gently with a soapy washcloth is a lovely scratch. Antiseptic soaps keeps infection down.

Air dry afterward so that skin absorbs the moisture. Speed up evaporation and provide cooling relief by gently blowing on the rash with a fan or hair dryer set to cool.

Showers and Soaps

Use gentle pH-balanced castile, vegetable oil, and glycerin soaps.

Antiseptic soaps
- For thwarting infection in rash areas. Includes: eucalyptus, neem, rosemary, tea tree, thyme, a variety of evergreens.

Herbal soaps
- Can't go wrong with calendula, jewelweed, lavender, or oatmeal soaps.

Poison oak and ivy soaps
- Nicely alkaline with herbs for soothing skin and fighting infection.

Baking Soda Soap by Grandpa Brands
- Alkalizing with a lovely safe scratch from the gritty baking soda.

Calendula products by Weleda
- A line of potent calendula lotions, creams and oils. Those for babies are extra gentle on the skin.

Fels-Naptha by Purex/Dial Corp.
- As a rash treatment it's awful, a counterproductive counter-irritant. No longer made by Fels and Co., it doesn't even contain include naphtha, a petroleum solvent, anymore. It's just a particularly nasty tallow soap.

Old-Fashioned Oatmeal Soap by Grandpa Brands
- Soothing with enough oatmeal granules for a lovely safe scratch.

Poison Ivy/Oak Bar by All Terrain
- Anti-inflammatory plantain and soothing concentrated oats with a touch of drying from antiseptic neem and tea tree oils.

Poison Ivy Soap by Burt's Bees
- Lovely and super alkalizing, with jewelweed and oatmeal for soothing, and pine tar and tea tree oil to help thwart infection and dry up ooze.

Soaking Baths

A good soak in a tub does wonders. But you just won't believe how fabulous a hot tub feels at this point in the rash — the bubbly water, oxygenated from ozone or bleach, is a terrific scratch. The warm, heavily saline water of a sensory deprivation tank can also be divine. While a steam, rather than a soak, ozone saunas feel great and accelerate skin healing.

Acidic
- Add a pint or two of apple cider vinegar for a slightly acidic bath. The aroma is very weak so you don't smell like a pickle. But you can always add an aromatic essential oil like lavender.

Alkaline
- For a soothing alkaline bath toss a ½ cup of baking soda or a cup of powdered milk into the water.

Oatmeal
- Soothes the skin as well as PI inflamed nerves. Do it yourself: Grind oatmeal into a powder. Toss a cup in the tub or use a cheesecloth bag or old hosiery to contain it. Run hot running water to dissolve the oatmeal. Then run cooler water to make the bath warm. Add essential oils or tinctures from Stage 2 for increased effect. Be careful: the tub will be very slippery.

Active Naturals Skin Relief Bath Treatment or **Soothing Bath Treatment** by Aveno
- The oatmeal master of personal-care products with colloidal oatmeal, green oat extract, and even oat oil (who knew there was such a thing?). Leaves a light protective film on the skin. Easy to use and widely available.

Calendula Cream Bath by Weleda Baby
- Mmmm.

Soothing Organic Milk & Oat Bath by Aura Cacia
- Divine on the skin, especially Calming Chamomile and Restoring Helichrysum & Lemon Balm versions.

Kitchen Remedies
- Minerals
- Fruits and Vegetables

Moderately strong acids (low pH) or alkalines (high pH) applied to the PI rash can abate itching, as outlined in Practice Safe Scratch in the Your Rash Toolkit section. A few of the alkalines aid the rash in healing.

Minerals

Baking Soda
- Mix baking soda with enough water — or better yet, real witch hazel astringent — to create a poultice and slather it on. Or blend into a gauze compress. Add essential oils or tinctures from Stage 2 for more rash relief. (Instructions under Tinctures and Essential Oils, below.) Ground up Alka-Seltzer Gold (the aspirin-free version) will do in a pinch. Or make a concentrated Alka-Seltzer solution and dribble it on; bubbles provide a light scratch. Use only if lesions and blisters are not open.

Milk of Magnesia
- Soothing application of magnesium. Look for those without added sweetener, aspirin or antacid. The mint-flavored version aids with cooling. Or add a few drops of essential oils from Stage 2 to the regular version. Instructions under Tinctures and Essential Oils, below. Keep a bottle in the refrigerator and daub it on with cotton balls. Slather it on and wrap with gauze for overnight relief (and messy sheets).

Fruits And Vegetables

Most vegetables are in the neutral pH range, which is soothing like seawater.

- On the alkaline end are avocado, asparagus, broccoli, Brussels sprouts, garbanzo beans, lima bean, mushroom, olive (non-fermented), soybean, spinach, and summer squash.
- Honeydew melon is a rare alkaline fruit.
- Tofu is alkaline due to the calcium used in processing. Mash well and slather them on yourself.

Bring the skin's acid mantle back to its natural pH by rinsing afterward and not using skin products for a few hours to allow the natural skin oils and flora to restore. If the skin becomes too acidic or alkaline, its beneficial bacteria can't function, and if too alkaline is more susceptible to infections.

PLEASE READ THESE CAUTIONS

Do you feel sick from the rash? You may need immediate medical attention. Read the chapter When To See a Doctor — Fast! in the Rash Mastery section.

If there are open cuts or lesions, broken skin or blisters, or otherwise abraded skin, be extra cautious with topical products.

Read labels carefully for contraindications.

Always consult with a physician first if you are pregnant or nursing, on medications or supplements, or have an acute or chronic health condition.

All topical products can cause contact dermatitis. If skin becomes additionally dry, red, inflamed or itchy, stop using the product.

If you have sensitive skin, test prior to use by applying to a small area first and monitoring for skin reactions.

Section 5 / Chapter 3

Stage 2 – Cooling the Itch

Chapter Index
- Topical Earth
- Topical Herbs
- Water-Based Relief
- Kitchen Remedies

The rash is blooming and blisters are on the way. Do everything possible to slow that momentum down. Shrink, shrink, shrink. Severe skin inflammation equates with heat. The right cooling products can be extremely effective. The goal is not to be your itch's bitch.

Cool water and gentle breezes chill through evaporation. Strong aromatics can impart an intense cooling sensation as they evaporate, while also constricting and reducing swelling, especially when mixed in an astringent base such as witch hazel. And they're effective counter-irritants for the itch of poison oak and ivy (abbreviated in *Itchy Business* as PI).

Topical Earth
- Clays
- Minerals

Clays

Calamine Lotion by GSMS
- The old-fashioned kind. Enhance by adding a few drops of cooling essential oils: camphor (natural), cypress, eucalyptus, fir, peppermint, rosemary, spearmint, spruce, sarsaparilla. Instructions under Essential Oils, below.

Minerals: Magnesium

Milk of Magnesia, Original by Phillips
- Soothing application of magnesium. Look for those without added sweetener, aspirin or antacid. The mint-flavored version aids with cooling. Or add a few drops of essential oils from Stage 2 to the regular version. Instructions under Tinctures and Essential Oils, below. Keep a bottle in the refrigerator and daub it on with cotton balls. Slather it on and wrap with gauze for overnight relief (and messy sheets).

Topical Herbs
- Tinctures
- Sprays
- Hydrosols
- Lotions and Creams
- Essential Oils
- Powders, Pads, and Compresses
- Poultices

The top choices for cooling herbs include: camphor, eucalyptus, rosemary, sarsaparilla, most mints, many evergreen trees.

But the camphor found in drugstore products is not the pleasantly pungent extract of the Asian camphor laurel or kapur tree. Instead, it's a just plain awful refinement of turpentine. Don't be mean to your skin.

Tinctures

Tinctures are concentrated alcohol or glycerin-based herbal solutions in small bottles with dropper tops.

> Do you feel sick from the rash? You may need immediate medical attention. Read the chapter **When To See a Doctor – Fast!** in the Rash Mastery section.

Blend several drops with ¼ cup of plant, nut, or seed oil, or a light base such as aloe vera or glycerin, to create a cream or lotion.
- Aloe based-blends can freeze into ice cubes.

Dilute 1 teaspoon in ½ cup water, witch hazel, isopropyl (rubbing) or ethyl (drinking) alcohol to use as a spray or soak a compress.
- Saturate a washcloth, heat in the microwave, and apply for a healing safe scratch.
- If using a non-alcohol solution, freeze to create ice cubes.

Mix several drops into a paste of ¼ cup each bentonite clay and water, and thin with a base lotion, to create a calamine-type product.
Remember to breathe in the aroma for best effect.

Tinctures for direct application include:
- sarsaparilla.

Dilute in a base (directions above):
- camphor, cypress, eucalyptus, fir and other evergreens, mints such as peppermint and spearmint, rosemary

Dermal Health by HerbPharm
- Anti-inflammatory burdock, soothing sarsaparilla, and other herbs in an ethyl (drinking) alcohol and glycerin base.

Sprays

Great for rash patches that sprawl. Make your own sprays by blending alcohol tinctures with water, witch hazel, or isopropyl (rubbing) alcohol or ethyl (drinking) alcohol to create a spray; directions under Tinctures. Keep chilled in the refrigerator for added cooling effect. Remember to breathe in the aroma for best effect.

Anti-Itchy by Ojas Ayurveda
- A gently acidic base of apple cider vinegar and cooling grain alcohol infused with natural menthol crystals and calendula, plus a hit parade of skin-bliss essential oils: blue chamomile, chamomile (Roman), helichrysum, and lavender.

Be Gone Scratch-N-Itch by Washington Homeopathics
- A whopping amount of grindelia (17%) plus natural camphor in an ethyl (drinking) alcohol base. Brisk! Does not leave a protective film on skin, which some prefer.

Continuous Spray Poison Ivy Treatment by Walgreens
- Benzyl alcohol (10 %) plus synthetic camphor and menthol for cooling.

Ditch the Itch Spray by All Terrain
- With tea tree oil and neem, it's strong enough to grow hair on your chest. Somewhat numbing and an effective counter-irritant.

Poison Oak/Ivy Remedy by Ojas Ayurveda
- Very similar to Anti-Itchy, also includes cypress.

Soothing Oak & Ivy by Herb Pharm
- A potent and aromatic combination of grindelia, sassafras, and natural menthol in an ethyl (drinking) alcohol base moderated by glycerin. Superbly cooling. Leaves a surface film that is very protective

Hydrosols

A lightly fragrant water by-product of essential oil distillation. Apply directly to skin with a dropper or dispense as a spray. Remember to breathe in the aroma in for best effect. Keep in refrigerator for greater cooling.

Peppermint Hydrosol by Mountain Rose
- Amazingly cooling and refreshing.

Cucumber Hydrosol by Mountain Rose
- Super cooling and refreshing, plus you smell like a salad.

Rosemary Hydrosol by Mountain Rose
- Surprisingly subtle woodsy aroma.

Lotions and Creams

Lotions and creams are usually not as potent as tinctures or sprays, but keep the herbs on your skin longer. Make your own; directions under Tinctures and Essential Oils.

Calming Itch-Relief Treatment by Eucerin
- Colloidal oatmeal lotion with cooling menthol and soothing evening primrose oil.

Terrasil Itch, Rash & Pain Relief by Aidance Skincare
- A highly active space-age cream with oxygen-rich oxides of magnesium, silver, and zinc in a base of bentonite clay, jojoba oil, and beeswax. Graced by cooling oils of eucalyptus and peppermint oil, and a touch of silver for antiseptic.

Essential Oils

Powerful concentrated substances distilled from plants in small bottles with drip dispensers.

- *Blend a few drops with a ¼ cup of plant, nut or seed oil or a light base such as aloe vera or glycerin, to create a cream or lotion.*
- *Dilute a few drops in ½ cup water, witch hazel, isopropyl (rubbing) or ethyl (drinking) alcohol to use as a spray or soak a compress.*
- *Mix several drops into a paste of ¼ cup each bentonite clay and water, and thin with a base lotion, to create a calamine-type product.*

Remember to breathe the aroma in as well for best effect.

Cooling essential oils include:
- camphor, cypress, eucalyptus, fir and other evergreens, mints such as peppermint and spearmint, rosemary, sarsaparilla

Powders, Pads, and Compresses

Pre-moistened pads are like ready-made compresses for applying to skin. Or soak fabric pieces such as gauze or cotton and apply as a compress. Some may be held in place by medical tape or gauze wrap.

Baby Powder by Averi Naturals
- Handy if skin is too tender to touch. Arrowroot powder and zinc oxide powder, plus calendula and lavender.

Extra Strength Triple Action Medicated Body Powder by Gold Bond
- Talc with zinc oxide plus eucalyptol, menthol, and thymol. So helpful when the skin is too tender to touch.

SuperHazel Medicated Astringent Pads by Thayers
- Cooling power from eucalyptol and peppermint oil, plus soothing calendula in a witch hazel, grain alcohol, and aloe vera base.

Cool Off Towelettes by Cool Off
- Large pre-moistened wipes designed to create comfort in hot weather. Stays moist for a long time. Base of witch hazel and isopropyl (rubbing) alcohol, glycerin, and aloe vera, with cooling lemon and menthol, chamomile and evening primrose for skin, astringent white tea, and other botanicals.

Poultices

Ground up plant matter moistened and slathered on skin.

Quick and easy poultice:
- herb tea bags. Drink the tea, apply the bag.

Cooling herbal teas include:
- ginger, peppermint.

Water-Based Relief

- Showers and Soaps
- Soaking Baths

Frequently washing with the right soaps, and occasional soaks in a tub, can greatly relieve the PI rash. Water softens crusty parts of the rash and moves dead skin cells away so new ones can arise. Rubbing gently with a soapy washcloth is a lovely scratch. Antiseptic soaps keep infection down. Air dry afterward so that skin absorbs the moisture. Speed up evaporation and provide cooling relief by gently blowing on the rash with a fan or hair dryer set to cool.

Showers And Soaps

Use gentle pH-balanced castile, vegetable oil, and glycerin soaps.

Antiseptic soaps
- For thwarting infection in rash areas while being cooling as well. Includes: eucalyptus, neem, rosemary, tea tree, thyme, a variety of evergreens.

Herbal soaps
- Can't go wrong with cooling eucalyptus, mint or rosemary soaps.

Medicated Poison Ivy Cleansing Formula by Ivarest
- High-suds detergent with menthol. Very brisk, very drying.

Soaking Baths

A good soak in a tub does wonders. But you just won't believe how good a hot tub feels at this point in the rash — the bubbly water, oxygenated from ozone or bleach, is a terrific scratch. The warm, heavily saline water of a sensory deprivation tank can also be divine. While a steam, rather than a soak, ozone saunas feel great and accelerate skin healing.

Aromatherapy Mineral Bath, Clearing Eucalyptus by Aura Cacia
- Clear sinuses!

Aromatherapy Mineral Bath, Refreshing Peppermint by Aura Cacia
- Brisk and skin stimulating.

Cold and Flu Bath by Abra
- Highly aromatic with natural camphor, eucalyptus, menthol, rosemary, sage, and tea tree oils. Clear sinuses are a side benefit of this bath.

Therapeutic Herbal Bath by Olbas
- Enough peppermint, eucalyptus, and evergreen oils to turn you into a popsicle. Makes bubbles!

Kitchen Remedies

Fruits And Vegetables

Cucumbers are cooling. Mash and slather. Alkaline fruits and vegetables good for skin treatments include avocado, honeydew melon, spinach, and summer squash. Tofu is alkaline due to the calcium used in processing. Pulp from juicing machines is excellent for this, plus you get the body-alkalizing benefit of the juice.

For information on PI in the news and updates on products, please visit the book website:

WWW.ITCHY.BIZ

Section 5 / Chapter 4

Stage 3 – Constricting the Blisters

Chapter Index
- Topical Earth
- Witch Hazel
- Other Astringents
- Salicylic Acid
- Topical Herbs
- Water-Based Relief

Stage 3 of the rash is nasty, nasty, nasty. Bullae bloom into blisters. Lymph fluid mixes with sloughed off skin and makes a disgusting crust. Blood vessels leak plasma that makes the rash area swell. Edema is so bad it stretches skin painfully taunt. Everything is sticky wet. The itch is very nervy and extremely intense, yet tender blistered skin prohibits all but the gentlest of rash treatments and safest of scratches — the perversity of poison oak and ivy (abbreviated in *Itchy Business* as PI).

Prevent the disgusting crust by washing often with tonifying soaps. Tighten up flabby blood vessels with tannin or herbal or mineral astringents. Drain edema-stricken tissues. Cold temperatures at this stage can help immensely. Seriously, find a walk-in freezer. It will feel so good.

Topical Earth

Minerals: Aluminum

Nothing tightens up and dries like aluminum. That's why it's part of most antiperspirants. It also inhibits nerve sensitivity, relieving itch. But it has a bad health reputation and chronic use can be terrible for you. Occasional applications are fine, especially since aluminum's astringent and itch-relief power is so strong. Aluminum chlorohydrate, highly effective and once a deodorant staple, is falling out of favor. The scramble is on to find formats of aluminum that lock out the metal's toxic qualities while allowing its good side to come through.

> The abbreviation "PI" refers to both poison oak and poison ivy.

Body Deodorant Spray by Crystal
- Based on potassium alum and meant for thicker body skin rather than thin underarm skin, so it penetrates better. Use lightly. Store in the refrigerator for added cooling.

Domeboro Astringent Solution
- Based on Burow's solution for eye problems, Domeboro comes as packets of aluminum sulfate tetradecahydrate and calcium acetate monohydrate. Mix with water to create a solution to rinse rash or soak skin compresses.

TriCalm Steroid-Free Hydrogel by TriCalm
- Aluminum acetate (0.2%) in a thin, fast-absorbing, non-greasy synthetic base. To thicken it up and add cooling oomph, store in the refrigerator.

Natural Confidence Deodorant Crystal Roll-On by Tom's of Maine
- Based on potassium alum from aluminum recycling operations and zinc citrate. Store in the refrigerator for added cooling.

Witch Hazel
- Astringents
- Powders, Pads, and Compresses

The wood of the modest witch hazel tree is famed for its astringent qualities that constrict and firm up skin. It strengthens the surface proteins of skin cells, forming a protective layer, and accelerates healing. Be picky about your brands. Many are primarily isopropyl (rubbing) alcohol. Make sure the solution is at least 75% witch hazel.

> **PLEASE READ THESE CAUTIONS**
>
> Do you feel sick from the rash? You may need immediate medical attention. Read the chapter When To See a Doctor — Fast! in the Rash Mastery section.
>
> If there are open cuts or lesions, broken skin or blisters, or otherwise abraded skin, be extra cautious with topical products.
>
> Read labels carefully for contraindications.
>
> Always consult with a physician first if you are pregnant or nursing, on medications or supplements, or have an acute or chronic health condition.
>
> All topical products can cause contact dermatitis. If skin becomes additionally dry, red, inflamed or itchy, stop using the product.
>
> If you have sensitive skin, test prior to use by applying to a small area first and monitoring for skin reactions.

Astringents

Soak cotton pads or balls and apply to skin or use as a compress. Speed up evaporation and provide cooling relief by gently blowing it with a fan or hair dryer set to cool.

Cucumber Witch Hazel Toner by Thayers
- Alcohol-free with soothing aloe vera. Smell like a salad! Also comes in plain and lemon versions.

Original Witch Hazel Astringent by Dickinson's
- Tighten up, baby!

Witch Hazel Extract by Mountain Rose
- Stout! Double distilled 86% witch hazel extract, plus 14% grain alcohol.

Powders, Pads And Compresses

Pre-moistened pads are like ready-made compresses for applying to skin. Or soak fabric pieces such as gauze or cotton and apply as a compress. Some may be held in place by medical tape or gauze wrap. In a pinch, you can use hemorrhoid-cleaning pads based on witch hazel as compresses.

Baby Powder by Averi Naturals
- Handy if skin is too tender to touch. Arrowroot and zinc oxide powders, plus calendula and lavender.

Cool Off Towelettes by Cool Off
- Large pre-moistened wipes designed to create comfort in hot weather. Stays moist for a long time. Base of witch hazel and isopropyl (rubbing) alcohol, glycerin, and aloe vera, with cooling lemon and menthol, chamomile and evening primrose for skin, astringent white tea, and other botanicals. Good for a compress covering a wide area.

Hazelets Witch Hazel Pads by T.N. Dickinson
- Brisk with 14% alcohol.

Original Witch Hazel Astringent Pads by Thayers
- Alcohol-free with soothing aloe vera.

Original Witch Hazel Refreshingly Clean Cleansing Cloths by Dickinson's
- Like a baby wipe, but soaked in witch hazel. Good for a compress covering a wide area. Alcohol-free.

SuperHazel Medicated Astringent Pads by Thayers
- Cooling power from eucalyptol and peppermint oil, plus soothing calendula in a witch hazel, grain alcohol, and aloe vera base.

Other Astringents

Fresh-Clean Astringent, Sensitive Skin Water by Sea Breeze
- Clove and eucalyptus oils, plus camphor, in an ethyl (drinking) alcohol base.

Natural Acne Solutions Clarifying Toner by Burt's Bees
- Naturally derived salicylic acid from willow bark, in an ethyl (drinking) alcohol base, with extracts of goldenseal, lemongrass, and witch hazel.

Salicylic Acid

- Sprays
- Astringents
- Lotions and Creams
- Soaps

Salicylic acid is used in many acne products to minimize pores and dry up zits. It can be a highly effective astringent and counter-irritant while at the same time encouraging the skin to slough off dead cells. It can also sting like the dickens, making it a counter-irritant for the hearty. Salicylic acid products labeled for sensitive skin will aggravate the rash less. Most salicylic acid is synthetic. Natural salicylic acid from willow bark is in Other Astringents, above.

Sprays

Great for rash patches that sprawl. Keep chilled in the refrigerator for added constricting effect.

Body Acne Treatment Spray by Nature's Cure
- That rare find of 2% salicylic acid in a more-or-less natural base of aloe vera and witch hazel, plus extracts of burdock, calendula, chamomile (German), echinacea, and willow bark.

> Practice safe scratch! Learn how in the Your Rash Toolkit section.

Astringents

Clear Pore Oil-Controlling Astringent by Neutrogena
- Salicylic acid (2%) in an isopropyl (rubbing) alcohol base, with aloe vera plus chamomile and witch hazel extracts.

Essentials Deep Cleaning Toner, Sensitive Skin by Clean & Clear
- Salicylic acid (2%) in an isopropyl (rubbing) alcohol base with a touch of aloe.

Lotions and Creams

Lotions and creams are usually not as potent as tinctures or sprays, but keep the compound on your skin for longer.

Advantage Mark Treatment by Clean & Clear
- Salicylic acid (2%) in a glycerin, isopropyl (rubbing) alcohol, and aloe vera gel base.

Clear Skin Acne Control Gel by Yes to Tomatoes
- Another rare find of 2% salicylic acid in a more-or-less natural base featuring aloe vera and (of all things) tomato extract.

Oil-Free Dual Action Moisturizer by Clean & Clear
- Salicylic acid (.5%) in a synthetic base.

Soaps

Body Clear Body Wash by Neutrogena
- Salicylic acid (2%) in a synthetic base, with infusions of chamomile and aloe.

Clear Skin Acne Control Gel Cleanser by Yes to Tomatoes
- Salicylic acid (1%) and tomato extract in a mostly natural soap base.

Oil-Free Acne Wash by Neutrogena
- Salicylic acid (2%) in a synthetic base with touches of chamomile and aloe.

Topical Herbs

- Sprays
- Lotions and Creams
- Poultices

Sprays

Great for rash patches that sprawl. Make your own sprays by blending alcohol tinctures with water, witch hazel, or isopropyl (rubbing) alcohol or ethyl (drinking) alcohol; directions under Tinctures. Keep chilled in the refrigerator for added cooling effect. Remember to breathe in the aroma for best effect.

Ditch the Itch Spray by All Terrain
- With tea tree oil and neem, it's strong enough to grow hair on your chest. Somewhat numbing and an effective counter-irritant.

Ivy-Dry Spray by Ivy-Dry
- Ivy-dry blend of benzyl alcohol, zinc acetate, and synthetic camphor and menthol, plus colloidal oatmeal, aloe vera and vitamin E to buffer. Very drying and numbing; can aggravate rash if overused.

Poison Ivy/Oak Spray by All Terrain
- Kaolin clay and zinc oxide in a handy spray with antiseptic neem and tea tree oils.

Rash Relief Spray by Tecnu
- Calendula, grindelia, and plantain in a glycerine and ethyl (drinking) alcohol base. Available at most drugstores. Also contains astringent green tea extract, antiseptic tea tree and white thyme oils, and cooling menthol. Amazing product. Moderates skin reactions of many kinds. Leaves a slight protective film on the skin. Grindelia's sharp, resinous aroma is the smell of relief. Do not confuse with the most famous Tecnu product, its Outdoor Skin Cleanser, which should not be used once the rash erupts.

Lotions and Creams

Lotions and creams are usually not as potent as tinctures or sprays, but keep the herbs on your skin longer. Make your own; directions under Tinctures and Essential Oils.

Be Gone Scratch-N-Itch Lotion by Washington Homepathics.
- A whopping amount of grindelia (17%) plus natural camphor in an ethyl (drinking) alcohol base. Brisk! Does not leave a protective film on skin, which some prefer. Incredibly cooling.

Sitting Pretty Balm by Mountain Rose
- A rare instance of a hemorrhoid balm that works on constricting other inflamed blood vessels. Yarrow, St. John's wort, witch hazel and more in an olive oil and beeswax base.

Poultices

Ground up plant matter moistened and slathered on skin.

Black tea
- Steep a cup of black tea. Apply the spent bag to the rash. Great source of astringent tannin for blisters.

Cilantro
- A slathering of mashed up cilantro on the skin can be soothing and help drain excess fluid from tissues. Available in grocery store produce sections. First use a tomato for acidic itch relief, follow with a smear of avocado to soothe, mix in cilantro — voila, guacamole!

Water-Based Relief

Frequently washing with the right soaps, and occasional soaks in a tub, can greatly relieve the PI rash. Water softens crusty parts of the rash and moves dead skin cells away so new ones can arise. Rubbing gently with a soapy washcloth is a lovely scratch. Antiseptic soaps keep infection down. Air dry afterward so that skin absorbs the moisture. Speed up evaporation and provide cooling relief by gently blowing on the rash with a fan or hair dryer set to cool.

Showers and Soaps

Foaming Facial Wash by Dickinson's
- Super brisk witch-hazel wash! No coffee needed after this.

Ivy-Dry Soap by Ivy-Dry
- Soap with Ivy-dry blend of benzyl alcohol, zinc acetate, and synthetic camphor and menthol, plus colloidal oatmeal, aloe vera, and vitamin E to buffer.

Pine Tar Soap by Grandpa's
- The rare creosote-free pine tar oil soap, very drying and antiseptic.

Poison Ivy/Oak Bar by All Terrain
- Anti-inflammatory plantain and soothing concentrated oats with a touch of drying from antiseptic neem and tea tree oils.

Poison Ivy Soap by Burt's Bees
- Lovely and super alkalizing, with jewelweed and oatmeal for soothing, and pine tar and tea tree oil to help thwart infection and dry up ooze.

Witch-Hazel Soap by Grandpa Brands
- Gentle soap with light astringent properties.

For information on PI in the news and updates on products, please visit the book website:

WWW.ITCHY.BIZ

Section 5 / Chapter 5

Stages 2 and 3 – Analgesics for Pain Relief

Chapter Index
- Sprays
- Lotions and Creams

The big bomb of itch relievers for poison oak and ivy (abbreviated in *Itchy Business* as PI) is topical analgesics like lidocaine, supplanting long-time benzocaine. They have one motto: Shut this PI party down! The 'caines interfere with skin nerves sending pain or itch messages. They act fast and reliably. They also dry your skin to Hades.

But when the 'caine wears off, sometimes the rash comes roaring back in a very bad mood. The 'caines become less effective with repeated use, causing people to apply them more often than is safe, leading to highly irritated and sensitized skin that's prone to sunburn and PI rashes.

The FDA issued warnings that applying large amounts of these topical 'caines can lead to life-threatening side effects such as an irregular heartbeat and seizures. People became so aestheticized they fell into comas. Inhaled (even accidentally) into interior mucous membranes like the throat, a potentially serious blood condition called methemoglobinemia can result.

> The abbreviation "PI" refers to both poison oak and poison ivy.

You've got options:
- Pramoxine hydrochloride (HCI) is a strong anesthetic, but not as problematic as lidocaine. On sensitive skin it can cause a range of freakouts from redness to hives, even increased itching.
- Benzyl alcohol gives a lovely light numbing while also being briskly cooling.
- Benzalkonium chloride is an antiseptic with a slight numbing quality.

Be safe. Read all package warnings and directions. Rub analgesic creams in lightly and use sprays when possible. If you are pregnant, nursing, on medications, or have a chronic health condition, always consult a physician first. Topical analgesics are not for use on children.

Sprays

Continuous Spray Poison Ivy Treatment by Walgreens
- Benzyl alcohol (10 %) plus menthol and camphor for cooling.

Wound Wash by Simply Saline
- Sterile saline solution with 0.13% benzalkonium chloride, moderated by aloe vera. Excellent on lesions.

Lotions and Creams

Anti-Itch Cooling Gel For Kids by Benadryl
- Benzyl alcohol cools itch in a big way, plus a touch (0.45%) of synthetic camphor to be sure. Contains no diphenhydramine antihistamine.

Anti-Itch Lotion by Gold Bond
- Synthetic base 0.5% menthol and 1% pramoxine hydrochloride amped up with aloe vera and colloidal oatmeal, plus 5% dimethicone that leaves a protective film on skin.

Anti-Itch Lotion, Sensitive, Fragrance-Free by Sarna
- Brisk benzyl alcohol base with 1% pramoxine hydrochloride.

CalaGel Medicated Anti-Itch Gel by Oak-N-Ivy
- A combination of 2% diphenhydramine antihistamine (not effective on PI) and 15% benzethonium chloride (yowsa!) with a touch of skin protecting zinc acetate.

First Aid Gel by Tecnu
- Numbing benzethonium chloride (0.20%) and even more numbing lidocaine (2.5%) in a synthetic base with a touch of allantoin for skin healing. When you just want to beat the rash into submission.

Medicated Calamine Lotion by Good Sense
- Blends calamine with 1% pramoxine hydrochloride.

Poison Ivy Itch Cream by Ivarest
- Contains bentonite and calamine, which is helpful, and benzyl alcohol for good itch relief. Then a host of ingredients either ineffective (antihistamine) or not healthy for skin (synthetic camphor, dyes) or too heavy (petroleum jelly, lanolin).

Soothe-It by SatisPHARMA
- Colloidal oats, oat oil, calamine, and aloe, plus soothing magnesium, serve as a base to a fascinating approach to itching. The theory is that if a nerve ending attracts a positive ion, it has a negative charge. Multivalent cations of sodium and potassium are used to confuse nerves. But also contains lidocaine and benzethonium chloride which numb nerves. Huh?

PLEASE READ THESE CAUTIONS

Do you feel sick from the rash? You may need immediate medical attention. Read the chapter When To See a Doctor — Fast! in the Rash Mastery section.

If there are open cuts or lesions, broken skin or blisters, or otherwise abraded skin, be extra cautious with topical products.

Read labels carefully for contraindications.

Always consult with a physician first if you are pregnant or nursing, on medications or supplements, or have an acute or chronic health condition.

All topical products can cause contact dermatitis. If skin becomes additionally dry, red, inflamed or itchy, stop using the product.

If you have sensitive skin, test prior to use by applying to a small area first and monitoring for skin reactions.

Section 5 / Chapter 6

Stage 4 – Repairing the Skin

Chapter Index
- How to Repair Your Skin
- Topical Herbs
- Water-Based Relief

Finally, the rash of poison oak and ivy (abbreviated in *Itchy Business* as PI) is over, but your work is not through. The cytotoxic devastation from the PI is deep in the dermis. Blisters peel and expose thin, tender outer skin that needs protection. Cells must start forming new skin one microscopic layer at a time.

Don't skip past Stage 4. The astringents for blistery Stage 3 squeeze your skin to desert dryness. That itch you think is lingering PI rash may be extremely dry skin screaming at you for moisturizer. Plus you don't want scars forming at lesion and blister sites.

How to Repair Your Skin

The aim of Stage 4 is four-fold (imagine that): rebuild moisture, repair capillaries, restore collagen, and regenerate skin.

The only moisture that skin accepts is water. Moisturizers simply make sure it stays there. They come in two primary flavors:

- Emollients prevent moisture evaporation by coating the skin. Examples are oils from nuts, seeds, and plants, plus a plethora of synthetic emollients.
- Humectants attract moisture to skin and can make you feel sticky in humid conditions. Glycerin (natural and synthetic) and aloe are humectants.

Most moisturizers are a mix of the two. Gels and serums are less heavy than lotions and creams, something men usually prefer.

Rash redness results from broken capillaries, so blood vessel tonifiers excel such as burdock and horse chestnut (my favorite). To facilitate capillary healing, use only lightweight products that allow the rash area to breathe easily, rather than ones based on lanolin, mineral oil or petroleum jelly. Products for extra dry skin may be too heavy.

Damage from the PI rash extends into the collagen-rich dermis layer of the skin. As skin layers re-establish they need a smooth base to lay new cells upon. Plumping it back up helps prevent scars. Topical vitamins C and E also help prevent scarring.

Those who use fancy facial products will recognize the concepts of repairing capillaries, restoring collagen, and generating new skin cells. In Stage 4, high-class cosmetics are your friend. Look for products with naturally derived compounds allantoin, bisabolol, hyaluronic acid, matricaria, panthenol, and squalene. Avoid any product meant to tighten pores or exfoliate, or are based on alcohol or astringents.

Use lighter treatments during the day and slather up to restore in the evening. Overnight skin creams tend to be heavier and more rejuvenating. Just give up on having clean sheets for a while.

Many of the products for Stage 2 calming will work for Stage 4. Except alkalizing is not needed now. Instead seek balanced pH products that will restore the skin's acid mantle and help defend against infections.

For information on PI in the news and updates on products, please visit the book website:

WWW.ITCHY.BIZ

Topical Herbs

- Tinctures
- Sprays
- Hydrosols
- Facial Products
- Botanic Oils
- Lotions and Creams
- Essential Oils

Calendula, chamomile, and helichrysum are the stars here. Comfrey, a mainstay in "green salves," is high in allantoin.

Tinctures

Tinctures are concentrated alcohol or glycerin-based herbal solutions in small bottles with dropper tops.

Blend several drops with ¼ cup of plant, nut, or seed oil, or a light base such as aloe vera or glycerin, to create a cream or lotion.

- *Aloe based-blends can freeze into ice cubes.*

Dilute 1 teaspoon in ½ cup water, witch hazel, isopropyl (rubbing) or ethyl (drinking) alcohol to use as a spray or soak a compress.

- *Saturate a washcloth, heat in the microwave, and apply for a healing safe scratch.*
- *If using a non-alcohol solution, freeze to create ice cubes.*

Mix several drops into a paste of ¼ cup each bentonite clay and water, and thin with a base lotion, to create a calamine-type product.

Remember to breathe in the aroma for best effect.

Tinctures suitable for topical application include:
- comfrey, sassafras.

Dilute in a base (directions above):
- Ultra soothing and gentle for children: calendula, chamomile, oats.
- Super soothers: jewelweed (orange), lavender (true), plantain.
- Blood vessel tonifier: burdock, horse chestnut.

Dermal Health by HerbPharm
- Anti-inflammatory burdock, soothing sarsaparilla, and other herbs in an ethyl (drinking) alcohol and glycerin base.

Sprays

Great for rash patches that sprawl. Make your own sprays by blending alcohol tinctures with water, witch hazel, or isopropyl (rubbing) alcohol or ethyl (drinking) alcohol; directions under Tinctures. Keep chilled in the refrigerator for added cooling effect. Remember to breathe in the aroma for best effect.

Hydrosols for making into skin restorative sprays include:
- calendula, chamomile (German), lavender.

Tinctures for making into skin restorative sprays include:
- burdock, calendula, cilantro, chamomile (German), comfrey, grindelia, jewelweed (orange), lavender (true), oats (green), plantain, sassafras.

After Shower Moisture Spritz by Skin Free
- Greatness. Olive seed oil (odorless!) and sweet almond oil with vitamin E.

Calendula Spray by Hyland's
- Non-alcohol base and wonderfully spunky at 22% extract. Proof that God loves us.

CapriClear Spray-On Moisturizer
- More greatness. Nothing but coconut oil without scents, dyes or preservatives in a quick-absorbing spray.

Wild Rose Facial Toner by Mountain Rose
- Based on lavandin (lavender hybrid) hydrosol and calendula extract, with carrot seed oil and essential oils of helichrysum and lavender.

Hydrosols

A lightly fragrant water by-product of essential oil distillation. Apply directly to skin with a dropper or dispense as a spray. Remember to breathe in the aroma in for best effect.

Chamomile Hydrosol by Mountain Rose
- Super cooling and refreshing, penetrates deeply into the skin.

Helichrysum Hydrosol by Mountain Rose
- Ultra soothing with an undefinable woody-herbal aroma.

Facial Products

Pricier than body lotions and creams, but often more potent.

Baby Derma White Mallow Face Cream by Weleda
- Coconut oil, sesame, and sweet almond oil, with borage oil and white mallow.

Daytime Argan Facial Oil Serum by Aura Cacia
- Sunflower, jojoba, and argan oil, with carrot seed oil and essential oils of helichrysum and patchouli. Effective and man friendly.

Facial Serum, Geranium by Mountain Rose
- Macadamia nut, jojoba, and argan oil base, with carrot seed oil and essential oils of geranium, palmarosa, and rosemary.

Hyaluronic Acid Rehydrating Serum or **Night Crème** by derma e
- Packed with hyaluronic acid, allantoin, and vitamin C.

Iris Hydrating Night Cream by Weleda
- Sweet almond oil, beeswax, and shea butter with extracts of iris root, chamomile, and calendula.

Botanic Oils

As simple as it gets: oils extracted from herb seeds that are high in gamma-linolenic fatty acids (GLA) or a carrier oil infused with herbs. Oils, for sounding oily, often absorb rapidly. Remember to breathe the aroma in as well for best effect.

Argan (Argania spinosa)
- It's a Moroccan gourmet oil, it's a cosmetic, it's argan oil, pressed from kernels of the argan tree. But use the unroasted, fast absorbing, beauty product. Argan is rich in natural vitamin E, squalene, and GLA. Use the de-odorized versions or ready yourself for a trippy aroma.

Borage (Borago officinalis)
- Super rich in GLA. Pleasant aroma. Avoid during pregnancy.

Evening primrose (Oenothera biennis)
- Nicely rich in GLA. Pleasant aroma.

Mountain Rose Herbal Oils
- Calming oils for PI rash include: calendula, mullein, plantain.

Wild Rose Facial Oil (Rosa moschata)
- Essential oils of helichrysum and lavende infused in a base of rosehip, jojoba, and carrot seed oils, olive oil infused with calendula flowers, and vitamin E.

Lotions And Creams

Lotions and creams are usually not as potent as tinctures or sprays, but keep the herbs on your skin longer. Make your own; directions under Tinctures and Essential Oils.

Anti-Itch Cream by Honeymark
- Manuka honey, jojoba and sunflower oils, cocoa and shea butters, colloidal oatmeal and aloe vera. Infused with extracts of chamomile, comfrey, echinacea, goldenseal, and lavender, graced by allantoin and bisabolol.

Borage Therapy Dry Skin Lotion by Shikai
- Aloe vera, safflower seed oil, and glycerite base, with jojoba and borage seed oil.

Califlora cream by Boericke & Tafel
- Nicely strong with calendula.

Horse Chestnut Cream by Planetary Formulas
- Horse chestnut with other herbal blood vessel tonifiers including witch hazel, white oak, and myrrh.

Moisturizing Lotion, Enriching Collagen & Almond by Aubrey Organics
- Sweet almond, evening primrose, wheat germ, and jojoba oils, plus aloe vera and soluble collagen with peppermint and ylang ylang essential oils.

Restorative Secret Skin Oil by Mountain Rose
- Rosehip seed oil, calendula-infused oil, and vitamin E, with helichrysum and neroli essential oils.

Sensitive Daily Moisturizing Cream by Burt's Bees
- Sunflower seed oil base with a touch of zinc oxide and kaolin clay. Simple and serene.

Skin Relief Moisturizing Lotion by Aveeno Active Naturals
- Glycerin and shea butter with three kinds of activated oatmeal.

Weleda
- A line of potent calendula lotions, creams and oils. Those for babies are extra gentle on the skin.

Essential Oils

Powerful concentrated substances distilled from plants in small bottles with drip dispensers.
- *Blend a few drops with a ¼ cup of plant, nut or seed oil or a light base such as aloe vera or glycerin, to create a cream or lotion.*
- *Dilute a few drops in ½ cup water, witch hazel, isopropyl (rubbing) or ethyl (drinking) alcohol to use as a spray or soak a compress.*
- *Mix several drops into a paste of ¼ cup each bentonite clay and water, and thin with a base lotion, to create a calamine-type product.*

Remember to breathe the aroma in as well for best effect.

Blue chamomile (German)
- Famed blue skin oil found in superior beauty products for sensitive skin.

Helichrysum
- Ultra soothing with an undefinable woody-herbal aroma.

Lavender (true)
- Soothing aroma and gentle for children.

A sample essential oil blend for skin from Aromaceuticals.com:
- 1 ounce (2 tablespoons) aloe vera gel or juice
- ¼ teaspoon calendula-infused oil
- 3 drops blue chamomile (German)
- 3 drops helichrysum
- 6 drops lavender
- 5 drops cypress

Swab onto rash several times daily. For children make it half as strong.

Water–Based Relief
- Showers and Soaps
- Soaking Baths

Showers and Soaps

Use gentle pH-balanced castile, vegetable oil, and glycerin soaps.

Herbal soaps
- Can't go wrong with calendula, jewelweed, lavender, or oatmeal.

Antiseptic soaps
- For thwarting infection in rash areas. Includes: eucalyptus, neem, rosemary, tea tree, thyme, a variety of evergreens.

Calendula Soap by Weleda Baby
- Castile soap with calendula and chamomile.

Moisturizing Bar for Dry Skin by Aveeno
- Oatmeal soother.

Sulphur Soap by Braunfels Labs
- A hearty 10% sulfur in a vegetable-oil soap. Helps regenerate new skin cells and heal wounds.

Thylox Acne Treatment Soap by Grandpa Brands
- Sulfur (3%) in a rich vegetable-oil soap.

Soaking Baths

Calendula Cream Bath by Weleda Baby
- Mmmm.

Soothing Organic Milk & Oat Bath by Aura Cacia
- Divine on the skin, especially Calming Chamomile and Restoring Helichrysum & Lemon Balm versions.

PLEASE READ THESE CAUTIONS

Do you feel sick from the rash? You may need immediate medical attention. Read the chapter When To See a Doctor — Fast! in the Rash Mastery section.

If there are open cuts or lesions, broken skin or blisters, or otherwise abraded skin, be extra cautious with topical products.

Read labels carefully for contraindications.

Always consult with a physician first if you are pregnant or nursing, on medications or supplements, or have an acute or chronic health condition.

All topical products can cause contact dermatitis. If skin becomes additionally dry, red, inflamed or itchy, stop using the product.

If you have sensitive skin, test prior to use by applying to a small area first and monitoring for skin reactions.

Section 5 / Chapter 7

Holistic: Treat the Body, Reduce the Rash

Chapter Index
- Vitamins and Supplements
- Make Your Gut Happy
- Alkalize Your Body
- Low Histamine Diet
- Acupuncture
- Ayurvedic
- Homeopathy

Holistic health considers the whole patient and focuses on treating the root cause of the ailment rather than symptoms. The philosophy is that creating a vibrant sense of general health enables the body's own healing capability to be supported. The goal is to proactively detect and treat health issues before they become acute.

Vitamins and Supplements

In holistic theory, vitamins and supplements that are anti-inflammatory, anti-oxidant and anti-allergy should discourage the over-reactiveness of the PI rash. Spread them out in two to three doses throughout the day. High-oxidant vegetable juice blends, often with acai and other exotic berries, provide these qualities and alkalize the body at the same time.

For information on PI in the news and updates on products, please visit the book website:

WWW.ITCHY.BIZ

Vitamins

Vitamin A (as beta-carotene)
- Anti-oxidant, promotes skin regrowth. Lowers the production of inflammatory immunoglobulins. 25,000 to 50,000 IU.

Vitamin C plus bioflavonoids
- Anti-allergy, anti-oxidant, immune support. Large amounts can cause diarrhea. 500 to 1000 mg.
-

Vitamin E (as tocopherols or mixed tocopherols, not dl-alpha tocopherols)
- Anti-inflammatory, anti-oxidant, restores skin elasticity. 500 IU.

Supplements

Enzymes (such as bromelain or Wobenzym)
- Anti-inflammatory when taken between meals.

Essential fatty acids (borage, evening primrose and flax oils, also fish oils)
- Inflammation soother.

Horse chestnut
- Can improve microcirculation and strengthen vein walls.

Quercetin
- A potent anti-allergy bioflavonoid. Check first for interactions with drugs and supplements, especially antibiotics, high blood pressure medicine, and chemotherapy.

Turmeric
- Yellow spice containing anti-inflammatory curcumin that cools inflamed tissues.

Make Your Gut Happy

To paraphrase an old Southern saying about mamas: If the gut ain't happy ain't nobody happy. An overly acidic stomach and cranky intestines may increase inflammation and feed the reactiveness of the PI rash. Be nice to your belly:

- Take acidophilus or probiotic supplements to get the good bacteria going.
- Digestive enzymes taken with food reduce the gut's reliance on acid to digest, and break down food more completely.
- Calm excess acidity with mineral supplements.

Alkalize Your Body

A highly acidic (low pH) body may be more reactive to the PI rash response. Eat to reduce acidity. Be super strict if just for a short time while the rash resolves. Carnivores and party animals — you can do it!

- No alcohol and coffee.
- No fried foods or animal fats.
- No animal protein and dairy products.
- No acidic foods like vinegar, tomatoes and citrus.
- Favor rice and oats over wheat.
- Drink many cups of mellow herb teas.
- Enjoy many bowls of miso or vegetable soup.
- Munch on nuts and seeds for essential fatty acids.
- Eat lots of leafy and green vegetables, especially as juices.

Low Histamine Diet

Histamine and allergy are a tight pair; itch is their love child. Histamine is contained in some animal products — think of shellfish and hives, for instance. A few fruits and vegetables stimulate the release of histamine. Fermenting, curing, aging, and smoking infuses food with reams of histamine. The logic is that avoiding these foods in the midst of a PI rash prevents you from throwing fuel on an already out-of-control fire.

Top histamine offenders to avoid:
- Alcohol
- Cheese
- Chocolate
- Egg whites
- Peanuts
- Shellfish
- Strawberries
- Tomatoes

Try to Stay Away From

Smoked, aged, cured and fermented foods
- Aged cheeses
- Alcohol (hard liquor), beer, champagne, cider, port, sherry, and wine
- Asian sauces such as fish, soy, and teriyaki
- Smoked or processed meats such as, bacon, lunch meats, and salami
- Sauerkraut and other fermented salads
- Vinegar and vinegar condiments such as hot sauce, ketchup, and mustard
- Yeasty baked goods such as bread and donuts

Cold-water fish
- Deep-sea fish such as halibut, mahi-mahi, and tuna
- Small fishes such as mackerel, sardines, anchovy, and herring
- Shellfish such as crab, lobster, and shrimp

Dairy products
- Soured products such as buttermilk and sour cream
- Fermented products such as yogurt and kefir
- Cheese, especially aged cheeses

Certain fruits
- Including bananas, citrus, kiwi, mango, papayas, pineapple, and strawberries

Certain vegetables
- Including avocado, eggplant, mushrooms, tomato, and spinach

Certain nuts
- Including cashews, peanuts, and walnuts

Acupuncture

Acupuncture is a facet of Traditional Chinese Medicine (TCM) which views the body in an entirely different way than western medicine. In TCM, meridians lace the body, connecting the major organs and glands. In China, Japan, and other Asian countries, where acupuncture has been practiced for thousands of years, it's considered mainstream.

Qi, or the animating energy of the body, runs through the meridians. They can be blocked or too open, have a stagnant flow or run too fast. The qi of an internal organ or gland can have qualities like hot or cold, dry or damp, yin or yang. The ultimate goal is a smooth orderly flow of qi and a balance of polarities. Very fine needles are inserted in those meridians to adjust qi and bring about balance and healing.

In just one acupuncture visit, I've had immense relief from PI rash, reducing the heat, swelling, and itch right away. I could literally feel the heat rise from the rash and watched the swelling rapidly subside.

A PI rash is usually considered a hot and wet condition in need of cooling and drying, though the patient's unique temperament can greatly influence that. The rash may be seen as having too much wind. Much focus is on the liver.

An acupuncturist will evaluate you with questions and diagnostics. Then you lay on a massage table, usually partially undressed, and the acupuncturist inserts very thin sterile needles at specific points. It does not hurt, barely a prick. Really. You relax for a while. Bring earbuds and music or a podcast. You're usually in and out in under an hour. Acupuncturists can also recommend TCM herbal supplements and dietary practices.

Acupressure uses a firm press of the hand to stimulate a meridian. For an allergy attack, apply pressure to webbed skin between the thumb and index finger, pressing somewhat close to the finger side of the skin. Hold for 2 minutes. Repeat frequently.

Locate an acupuncturist near you: acufinder.com, aaaomonline.org/search, or nccaom.org.

Ayurvedic

Ayurvedic medicine maintains there are doshas that indicate a person's physical temperament: kapha (slow, earth), pitta (moderate, water and fire), and vata (fast, air). A person is a combination of all three doshas, with one or two being most pronounced.

In Ayurvedic theory, the liver is deeply involved with fire in the body and most skin inflammation. With the heat of the PI rash and the wetness of blisters, the focus is usually on balancing pitta, but it depends on the patient. An Ayurvedic physician will usually recommend liver cleansing.

Locate an ayurvedic physician near you: ayurvedanama.org.

Homeopathy

A very simple way to describe the theory of homeopathy it is "like cures like," The logic goes that if a large dose of something would make someone ill, a minute dose of the same would cure by stimulating specific physiological responses. The homeopathic solution is dripped on sugar pills that are dissolved slowly under the tongue.

Weird, I know, yet for a lot of people it's just the trick. Germans are crazy about it. The usual dose is three to five sugar pellets or pills of the remedy under the tongue every two hours, increasing the time between doses as improvement arises.

Anacardium orientale or occ:
- Acute contact dermatitis. For Stage 1, 2 or 3.

Apis mell: Blisters.
- For Stage 2 or 3.

Graphites: Oozing;
- cracked skin, especially in skin folds. For Stage 3.

Rhus tox:
- For Stage 1.

Sulfur:
- Wound healing. For Stage 4.

Homeopathy is fairly nuanced stuff. Avoid smoking, drinking alcohol or coffee, or eating strong-flavored foods for a few hours before and after.

To find a homeopathic physician near you: homeopathic.org.

PLEASE READ THESE CAUTIONS

Do you feel sick from the rash? You may need immediate medical attention. Read the chapter When To See a Doctor — Fast! in the Rash Mastery section.

If there are open cuts or lesions, broken skin or blisters, or otherwise abraded skin, be extra cautious with topical products.

Read labels carefully for contraindications.

Always consult with a physician first if you are pregnant or nursing, on medications or supplements, or have an acute or chronic health condition.

All topical products can cause contact dermatitis. If skin becomes additionally dry, red, inflamed or itchy, stop using the product.

If you have sensitive skin, test prior to use by applying to a small area first and monitoring for skin reactions.

6

Identifying the Plant

Section Index
1. The American Axis of Itching
2. Know Your Adversary

"Leaves of three, let them be.
Berries white, poisonous sight.
Hairy vine, no friend of mine."

That might be a good summation of the identification basics for poison oak and ivy (abbreviated in Itchy Business as PI) — if only PI weren't so variable. There are four species of PI and each looks different. Some don't vine, and not all PI vines have hair. PI is a deciduous plant and "leaves of three" won't do you any good when they aren't there. Stems, berries, and roots have plenty of urushiol to give you a dandy rash.

To effectively identify the plant you must know your opponent as a PI ninja would. That means being aware of how it looks in all seasons and all regions. Most of all, you need to understand its growing habits so you can anticipate where it will be. Being able to recognize its lookalike imitators will reduce PI paranoia. Let's get to know the American Axis of Itching.

Section 6 / Chapter 1

The American Axis of Itching

Chapter Index
- Four Main Species and Where They Grow
- Poison Sumac: the Swamp Monster

Poison oak and ivy (abbreviated in *Itchy Business* as PI) are a fierce foursome of species. All species contain urushiol [oo-roo-**shee**-ohl], a vicious (to humans) allergen. Once thought to be part of the sumac family (*Rhus*), PI is now considered by most botanists to be in the larger cashew family (*Anacardiaceae*). Joining them is poison sumac and a bunch more nasty plants containing urushiol on other continents. Their genus is called *Toxicodendron*, which is botany speak for "poisonous tree." Now that's truth in labeling.

> The abbreviation "PI" refers to both poison oak and poison ivy.

Four Main Species & Where They Grow
- Eastern poison ivy
- Western poison oak
- Eastern poison oak
- Rydberg's poison ivy

Here's a great tip: In the fall PI turns in a bright array of yellow, orange and red. You'll see it in all kinds of places you didn't realize it was.

Red leaves on Eastern poison ivy

Eastern Poison Ivy (*Toxicodendron radicans*)

The most widespread of the quartet, if you're in the South or Midwest, this is your poison plant. There are at least six subspecies of *radicans* in the U.S. and they all look different. From the Latin for radiating, thus a plant with radiating stems which will form additional roots.

Eastern poison ivy

Radicans is a very ancient and persistent plant. Its ancestors were native to southern China and Taiwan some 80 million years ago. From there it spread over the Far East and Southeast Asia, arriving in North America so far in the past it's considered native here. Other domestic species of PI descended from *radicans*.

Growing Habits:
- *Radicans* grows up, down and around. A radicans vine can climb 150 feet or more and grow to over 5 inches thick. It exists as a shrub from 2 to 8 feet tall, and is even found in tree form.
- More often, *radicans* forms thickets of slender 3- to 4-foot stems that grow up from rhizomes. They look dangerously like tree saplings in the winter and are very springy, able to slap the urushiol deep into the skin.
- Extensive mats of roots, rhizomes, and surface vines develop that rock for erosion control, but are notorious for tripping people right into the *radicans*.

Eastern poison ivy stems - winter

Habitat:
- *Radicans* favors partial shade, though will grow weakly if the shade is deep. Open woods with dappled shade along creeks are its happy place. It takes full sunlight with

enough water, especially if the location affords a couple hours of shade a day. It prefers its roots to be cool and grows on the sides of structures and rocks so its roots can extend beneath.

Eastern poison ivy vines climbing tree

- Haunting every woods and creek corridor in the South and Midwest, you'll find it growing up or around almost every tree. Vines drape from the limbs and berries drop to create a groundcover of tiny plants. Older PI specimens can extend underground stems called rhizomes for 20 feet or more that sprout a plethora of 2- to 4-foot stems. A 365-degree poison sphere of radicans

Eastern poison ivy berries - summer

- You'll also find it growing on railroad tracks, roadsides, bridges and bluffs. It has a special love of abandoned buildings. It arises along fences and beneath powerlines, where resting birds deposit its drupes (berries).

Range:

- *Radicans* is found in the eastern coastal states from Maine to Florida, the entire South including Arkansas, Missouri, and the eastern parts of Oklahoma and Texas. It grows in the Midwest, Upper Midwest, and parts of the Great Plains states (except North Dakota). Just to be perverse, it grows in pockets of Arizona.

Range of Eastern poison ivy

- Outside of the U.S., *Radicans* is found in southern Canada, the Bahamas and Bermuda, and Mexico and Central America. Courtesy of dim-witted plant collectors, PI spread to Europe, Australia, and New Zealand but hasn't naturalized much.

Eastern poison ivy first leaf - early spring

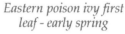

Eastern poison ivy bush

Eastern poison ivy berries - winter

Eastern poison ivy vines and dead leaves - late fall

Western Poison Oak
(Toxicodendron diversilobum)

Rugged and rowdy, *diversilobum* is very widespread. If you're in the woods west of the Rocky Mountains, this is your poison plant. Western poison oak can be so prevalent that it creates a namesake ecosystem, with dense thickets forming up to half the foliage in mature woods. Nobody logged or developed these areas, so they became havens for wildlife sensitive to human intrusion, such as the endangered Bell's Vireo.

Western poison oak - young

Growing Habits:

- *Diversilobum* refers to its chameleon-like ability to take diverse leaf styles and growing habits. A formidable plant, shrubs can tower at 10 feet or more and it makes trees. Thick vines can climb over 100 feet and can smother and kill even very large trees. These vines serve as conduits to move wildfire up tree trunks to the flammable crowns — horrifying!

Western poison oak with flowers

Habitat:

- A denizen of open mixed-evergreen forests, it takes hold on rocky slopes along creeks and canyons. It's able to grow in acidic soils, even amid chaparral and coastal sage scrub. It's shockingly drought tolerant.

Range:

- It grows in the western coastal states (except for deserts and high plateaus) from British Columbia down into Baja California, and eastward through the Sierra Nevada and Cascade mountain ranges.

Western poison oak berries - late fall

Range of Western poison oak

Western poison oak bush - fall

> Protect yourself from PI exposure with barrier creams, the right clothes, and to-go cleaners. Read about it in the Defending Yourself section.

Eastern Poison Oak (Toxicodendron pubescens)

A denizen of the Atlantic and Gulf coastal plains in the Southeast, *pubescens* is set apart by it downy foliage, stems, and berries — hence the species name. Fortunately, eastern poison oak favors areas where humans are not common. Broad thickets of pubescens spread for miles on shoreline sandbars and rugged riverbanks. It is to boaters as the Sirens of Greek mythology — ultra dangerous and nigh unavoidable.

Eastern poison oak

Growing Habits:

- Bushy with a well-lobed leaf, with everything covered in downy hairs. Never grows as a vine.

Eastern poison oak leaves

Habitat:

- Prefers more sunlight than other PI species and occurs in open forests, especially pine, and in scrub oak and pine savannas. It flourishes, even in full sunlight, along shorelines where it can receive abundant water. The species is tolerant of nutrient-poor, sandy, acidic, and saline soils. It is a survivor.

Eastern poison oak flowers

Range:

- *Pubescens* ranges all along the eastern coastal states from New Jersey to the northern part of Florida. It flourishes all throughout the Deep South, eastern parts of Texas and Oklahoma, and the Ozark Mountain regions.

Range of Eastern poison oak

Eastern poison oak berries

Rydberg's Poison Ivy *(Toxicodendron rydbergii)*

Also called western poison ivy, it's the mellowest of the PI species and prefers cooler temperatures.

Growing Habits:

- Rydberg's is a big-boned and bushy shrub though sparingly branched. Forms thickets of sapling-like 3- to 4-foot stems. It never vines, but does sort of scramble up tall slopes.

Rydberg's poison ivy

Habitat:

- It is drought tolerant yet can take short-term flooding. Able to flourish in full sunlight, it's also a denizen of mature woods. Often moves quickly into disturbed areas like logged forests. Accepting of dry and poor soils, it even grows in sand dunes, but doesn't like it extremely acid or alkaline. Best known for forming gnarly thickets on rocky expanses, subalpine talus slopes, canyon sides and vertical cliff faces, even in desert areas. Just when you think you've found a place where PI cannot grow, you'll encounter Rydberg's.

Range:

- Rydberg's prefers the chilly northern U.S. (except Alaska) and southern Canada, and extends down through the Rocky Mountains into northern Mexico. Its territory wraps around the Great Lakes and up into the New England states.

Range of Rydberg's poison ivy

Rydberg's poison ivy berries   *Rydberg's poison ivy - young*

Poison Sumac: The Swamp Monster

Poison sumac *(Toxicodendron vernix)* joins poison oak and poison ivy in the American Axis of Itching. Its toxicity knocks PI off the charts. Australian botanist Otto Frankel termed it the most poisonous plant in the U.S.

Poison sumac bush

Rydberg's poison ivy flowers

Growing Habits:
- Looking nothing like PI, the large, rangy shrub has 7 to 13 glossy leaves with downy undersides on a long stem. Smaller stems and leaves often have a red tint. Flower stems are several inches long.

Poison sumac flowers

Habitat:
- We're lucky that *vernix* primarily grows where humans don't go: swamps and peat bogs. But it does pop up in very wet or flooded soils

Range:
- Poison sumac is native to east of the Mississippi River, with a few pockets in Louisiana and East Texas. It favors the Deep South and New England, and also grows around the southern Great Lakes.

Range of Poison sumac

For the most extensive collection of photos showing PI in a variety of seasons and situations visit

WWW.POISON-IVY.ORG

For information on PI in the news and updates on products, please visit the book website:

WWW.ITCHY.BIZ

Poison sumac leaf - fall

Section 6 / Chapter 2

Know Your Adversary

Chapter Index
- The PI ID Basics
- Identifying PI in All Places and Seasons
- Innocent Imitators

Poison oak and ivy (abbreviated in *Itchy Business* as PI) is just ornery. Larger vines and shrubs tend to survive all but the worst extended droughts. Wildfires and forest fires don't much bother PI because of its underground rhizomes. It survives floods and long bouts of standing water. It will always be with us.

The PI ID Basics

Each of the species looks and grows differently, they sometimes grow together, and some even hybridize — an identification nightmare. You can know your regional species very well, but not recognize it in other areas.

A few things for sure about PI:
- Neither oak nor ivy
- A PI leaf consists of 3 leaflets (with rare exceptions of 5 and 7)
- Leaflets attach by a rachis (stalk), rather than direct to the stem, and the middle rachis is longer
- Leaves alternate on the stem, rather than in opposing pairs
- Never has thorns or tendrils

PI grows in all kinds of plant forms:
- Climbing vine
- Ground vine
- Shrub
- Tree

Yes, a tree. Specimens over 25 feet tall are on record.

Reminder: All parts of the PI plant are poisonous except nectar and pollen.

The leaves, from 2 to 6 inches long, have great variety:
- Round, oval, or slender shape
- Broadly or deeply ragged or lobed
- Rounded or tipped ends
- Smooth or broadly serrated margins (edges)

If you want to be completely sure a plant is PI, while wearing protective gear cut across a stem. Be sure to clean your knife afterward! Or bash a leaf against a piece of white paper. Wait a few minutes. If it's PI, the leaking urushiol [oo-roo-**shee**-ohl] will react to air and turn black.

For the most extensive collection of photos showing PI in a variety of seasons and situations visit *Poison-ivy.org*. If you deal with a lot of outdoor workers, visitors, or volunteers, the site's identification posters are a worthy investment.

Identifying PI In All Places and Seasons
- Leaf Shape
- Leaf Textue
- Leaf Color
- Stems
- Climbing vine
- Ground vine
- Roots and Rhizomes
- Blooms
- Berries

It's not enough to know the PI leaves. Some of the nastiest rashes come from encounters with PI vines and stems that are found sans leaves in the late fall, winter, and early spring. Those pretty berries? You definitely don't want to pick those.

Until PI gets large enough to implement its plan for world domination, it deviously blends in with other plants. The creeper or ground vine form of eastern

81

poison ivy is particularly bad about that. Those tactics are listed as Sneaky PI.

Leaf Shape

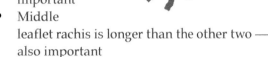

- A PI leaf consists of three conjoined leaflets
- Each leaflet attaches by a rachis (stalk), not directly to the stem — this is important
- Middle leaflet rachis is longer than the other two — also important
- Leaves alternate off the stem, not in pairs — way important
- The middle leaflet is generally larger and more symmetrical
- Leaflet tends to be oval with a slight tip, but can be long and slender, and the end can be round.
- Leaflet can be deep to shallowly lobed or even angularly ragged.
- Leaflet margins (edges) range from smooth to broadly serrated.
- Mature leaflets are 2 to 4 inches long though sometimes much bigger if conditions are prime
- Leaves attach to the stem by a 2- to 4-inch petiole (leaf stalk)
- Petiole clasps slightly around the stem
- A V or U-shaped scar is left on the stem when a petiole falls off

Exceptions:
- *PI on rare occasions has groups of 5 or 7 leaves.*
- *Western poison oak has extra leaves more often than other species.*
- *Poison oak leaves tend to be more rounded and deeply lobed.*
- *Eastern poison ivy can have slender leaves.*

> Protect yourself from PI exposure with barrier creams, the right clothes, and to-go cleaners. Read about it in the Defending Yourself section.

Leaf Texture

- The surface is often shiny or glossy.
- Leaf surface is usually smooth and flat, but can be rumpled or puckered.

Exceptions:
- *Eastern poison oak leaves have pale undersides with downy fibers.*
- *Western poison oak leaves tend to be very rumpled.*
- *PI grown in saline areas tends to pucker.*

Leaf Color

- Leaves often start out with a reddish tint in the spring and turn bright green.
- Summer leaves are deep green but occasionally tinged with yellow or orange.
- Leaves usually turn bright yellow, orange, or red in autumn.

Exceptions:
- *Western poison oak fall color is extremely and dependably red.*

Stems

- Bark is smooth and brownish gray.
- Often have hairy rootlets at the base, especially older plants.
- Smaller and younger stems sometimes have a touch of red to them.

Sneaky PI:
- Bare stems can look like innocent saplings. Absent-mindedly trailing a bare hand across stems comes back to haunt goofy people.

Exceptions:

- Eastern poison ivy stems from rhizomes tend to emerge from the soil at a slight angle.
- Eastern poison ivy stems are springy and tend to slap back after being pressed down, forcing the urushiol deep into the skin.
- Western poison oak is rather stoutly branched and less springy.
- Eastern poison oak stems are downy rather than hairy.

Climbing Vine

- PI vines never have tendrils or thorns.
- They tend to grow straight up trunks, rather than coiling around.
- Vines, especially those of eastern poison ivy, will ascend utility and fence poles, buildings and structures, shrubs and trees — essentially anything stationary and vertical.
- Older vines, particularly eastern poison ivy, can look like hairy rope and span 4 inches or more.

Sneaky PI:

- Thin vines of western poison oak and eastern poison ivy climb unseen in crevices of furrowed tree bark. To chainsaw or handle the trunk is to guarantee urushiol exposure. Burn the wood and you could land in the hospital from inhaling urushiol. Don't climb trees without protective gear and don't sit on fallen tree trunks. PI on the butt or groin is miserable. Never inhale or be downwind from bonfire or wildfire smoke.
- Vines can send out lateral branches that blend with the tree's own and are notorious for slapping people in the face.
- Vines will also grow out on a limb and drape down. You just don't expect to see PI descending from the sky.

Exceptions:

- Eastern poison oak does not climb at all.

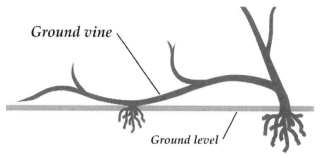

Ground Vine

- Thrives in forested areas, but can grow in full sunlight if somewhat shaded by other plants or structures.

Sneaky PI:

- Grows hidden in grass and groundcovers. Hike in sandals at your own peril.
- In the woods, blends in with harmless vines such as Virginia creeper.
- Grows on creek banks and leaches urushiol into the nearby water.

Exceptions:

- Eastern poison ivy acts as a ground vine more than other species.
- Eastern poison oak and western poison ivy does not vine at all.

Roots and Rhizomes

- Roots and rhizomes (underground stems) have a woody exterior and orange inner bark.
- Rhizomes mix with roots and sprout vertical stems.
- Both tend to be shallow — a major tripping hazard and a real danger of serious urushiol

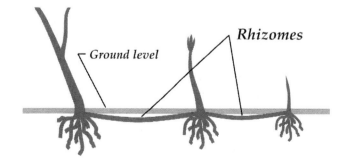

exposure if you fall.
- Roots and rhizomes (and surface vines in eastern poison ivy) form a network that can extend several yards around a main plant — great for erosion, but extremely difficult to eradicate.

Blooms

- Plants flower in late spring.
- 5 slender petals create ¼ inch flowers with a deep well.
- Color ranges from white to cream to light green.
- Blooms cluster on 3- to 6-inch stems that rise from the axil, where leaf stem meets the main stem.
- Emerges in mid spring, often well hidden by leaves.

Exceptions:
- *Not all PI plants make flowers, especially those in full shade.*

Berries

Eastern poison ivy berries

- Technically a drupe, a fleshy fruit around a single stone-like center, but we'll call them berries.
- Berries are about ¼ inch across covered by a papery thin skin with a waxy sheen.
- They start out bright green and turn white or cream if soil is rich, and gray or pale green if soil is poor.
- Urushiol resin canals are visible beneath the skin as black vertical lines.
- Berries mature by summer but are often not visible until leaf drop.
- They linger on the vine through winter, making for excellent wildlife food.

Exceptions:
- *Eastern poison oak has downy berries.*

Innocent Imitators

Being aware of PI lookalikes greatly reduces the panic factor. Plus there's no sense putting energy and money into exterminating something that's not PI.

The Top Imitators

Virginia creeper (*Parthenocissus quinquefolia*)
- This is the most frequent panic-inducer since it's a ground vine that occasionally climbs and gets hairy. Its new leaves are also reddish. It looks like creeping PI before the last two of its five leaflets unfurls. But it has jagged leaf margins (edges) and sometimes tendrils. Since they like the same habitats, Virginia creeper and eastern poison ivy sometimes grow together, adding to the sneak factor.

Virginia Creeper

- Distribution: Primarily in woodlands east of the Mississippi River in the U.S., extending into northern Mexico and southeastern Canada.

Box elder (*Acer negundo*)
- The saplings have lookalike leaves and the middle leaf has the proper rachis (stalk). The plant tends to seed thickly, creating so many offspring it appears to be a ground cover. They soon lose their bushiness and become obviously trees. But it's a panic until then.

Box Elder

- Distribution: Nationwide in moist areas, especially east of the Mississippi River, though not common in New England. In the west found only in areas with abundant water such as along creeks and lakes. Found in scattered areas of Canada, Mexico and Central America.

Additional Paranoia Inducers

Aromatic sumac *(Rhus aromatica)*
- Also called skunk or squaw bush, it can look a bit like bushy lobed forms of PI. But the triple leaves are small, and the center leaf tapers to the stem (no rachis), plus the berries are red.

Aromatic Sumac

- Distribution: Widespread in wooded areas east of the Mississippi River, plus Texas and the Great Plains states except North Dakota.

Blackberry family *(Rubus)*
- Wild versions also include dewberry, raspberry, and thimbleberry. Leaves are in groups of three and the middle leaves have a rachis. But leaf edges are finely toothed, stems have tiny thorns, and fruit is incorrect (though delicious).

Blackberry

- Distribution: In sunny areas primarily east of the Mississippi River, plus Texas and the lower and eastern Great Plains states, but are found in all states and Canada.

Bladdernut *(Staphylea trifolia)*
- Shrub with slender, oval, tipped leaves that grow in sets of three. But they join together at a center point with no rachis on the middle leaf, and has small white, bell-like flowers.

Bladdernut

- Distribution: Widespread in the Midwest, but found in the South, lower Great Plains states, parts of the East Coast, and eastern Canada.

Boston ivy *(Parthenocissus tricuspidata)*
- Leaves can have a red tint when young, and some are so deeply lobed they appear to be three leaves. Leaf margins are finely toothed and vines have tendrils.

Boston Ivy

- Distribution: Asia native planted extensively in sunny urban areas as a climbing vine to cover buildings façades. Has naturalized in the Midwest, East Coast, and parts of Canada.

Hop tree *(Ptelea trifoliata)*
- Also called wafer ash, this tree often grows as a shrub. It has look-alike leaves, but the center leaf tapers to the stem (no rachis) and the fruit is a seed with papery wings.

Hop Tree

- Distribution: Grows primarily in moist areas of the Midwest, Southeast and parts of Texas, Oklahoma, Arkansas, and the interior of Mexico, but is scattered throughout the Southwest and extends into eastern Canada.

Jack in the pulpit *(Arisaema triphyllum)*
- Low-growing perennial that grows in forests and is best known for its calla lily shaped bloom. The slender, oval, tipped leaves grow in sets of three, but they join together at a center point with no rachis on the middle leaf.

Jack in the Pulpit

- Distribution: Widespread in moist wooded areas east of the Mississippi River, plus Texas and the Great Plains states, and throughout the eastern half of Canada.

Sassafras (Sassafras albidum)

- A tree sometimes found as a shrub or thicket. One of its leaf shapes has three lobes, and another has notched leaf margins. Mostly its younger stages are mistaken for PI. The root beer and gumbo filé aroma definitely sets it apart from PI.

Sassafras

- Distribution: Widespread in deciduous forests east of the Mississippi River, plus Oklahoma, Arkansas, and the eastern parts of Texas.

For information on PI in the news and updates on products, please visit the book website:

WWW.ITCHY.BIZ

Defending Yourself

Section Index
1. Prevent Skin Contact
2. Prevent Secondary Exposure

Fear nature no more! From the previous section, Identifying the Plant, you can now spot all four species of poison oak and ivy (abbreviated in *Itchy Business* as PI) in its many plant-growing forms and in every season. As a PI ninja, you can even anticipate where it will grow, avoiding those "leaves of three" that you just don't see.

Take your PI ninja training a step further and learn how to stop urushiol [oo-roo-shee-ohl] from touching your skin. Effective clothing goes a long way and PI barrier creams can be downright amazing. But urushiol still gets on your clothes, tools, and pets, and from there it can spread everywhere, even back to your skin. But the right personal habits can stop that.

Section 1 / Chapter 1

Prevent Skin Contact

Chapter Index
- Barrier Lotions
- Protective Clothing
- Removing Nuclear Clothes
- Better Habits

The best way to protect yourself from PI is to keep something between you and the plant. The right clothes can do that, and skin barrier lotions can protect what's not covered.

Barrier Lotions

You remember to put on sunscreen and bug spray, right? Make a PI barrier lotion part of your outdoor preparations. The science of PI contact prevention has been fascinating. IvyBlock ruled for years with a groundbreaking organoclay compound that encapsulated urushiol — far superior to previous thick, sticky lotions. Now the king is Ivy X Pre-Contact Barrier with a sleek polymer approach that prevents penetration, similar to liquid bandages or skin shielding lotions, but unlike those actually effective against urushiol.

But don't go rolling in the PI patch just yet. PI ninja rule: Never get cocky. Barrier lotions can be overwhelmed by massive exposure. People extremely sensitive to PI may react if plant contact is firm.

PI barrier lotion tips:
- Read the instructions carefully.
- Go extra thorough on the joints and don't forget the ears.
- PI paranoid? Apply beneath clothing, especially lightweight textiles.
- Be sure to cover clothing gaps: the neck and between pants and socks, sleeves and gloves, shirt and pants.

Check your coverage after heavy activity and re-apply when it gets rubbed off. Be very careful since the barrier lotion may have urushiol resting atop it. Don't go hugging folks or leaning on walls and furniture. If you leave it on too long, any urushiol encountered will get down to its itchy business. Afterward, wash off the barrier lotion carefully with a high-surfactant soap and lots of warm running water, rinsing in a downward motion without splashing.

Ivy X Pre-Contact Barrier by CoreTex
- Described by the company as "ultimate in portable prophylaxis," they don't exaggerate. Ivy X is a superior product that works as a barrier against all poisonous plants. The gel goes to work immediately, and the film it leaves on the skin is thin and invisible.
- The secret of Ivy X is polyquaternium-11, a beige polymer film with quaternary ammonium centers and a strong positive charge. It's a common anti-static ingredient in cosmetics such as hairspray. Ivy X attaches tight tight tight to the skin, so much that it's extremely difficult for anything, even microscopic, to enter. Completely kick ass.
- Ivy X incorporates a lot of witch hazel, which seriously tightens up and strengthens skin surface, with plenty of aloe vera to make it mellow. Serious attention is paid to skin botanicals with white oak bark, St. John's Wort, and wild thyme. Comes in everything from individual wipes to gallon jugs, with the spray bottle being very handy.

Urushiol is a penetrating resin that operates on a molecular level. It scoffs with derision at these barrier attempts for their pathetic inadequacy:
- Liquid bandages or conventional skin-shielding lotions
- Spray deodorant with aluminum chlorohydrate
- Dimethicone skin protectant lotions
- Sunscreen with zinc oxide
- Colloidal oatmeal lotions
- Liquid rubber or latex
- Hair spray

Protective Clothing

Urushiol loves sweat. Your salty excretions take it for a joyride all over your body wherever sweaty clothing clings. Light, loose-fitting clothing is what you need over as much of your body as you can tolerate. That's hard in hot weather. As a Texan I know. And clothing is only a partial solution. Urushiol can still soak through. But fabric lessens the amount contacted and buys you vital time. Wash as soon as possible, instructions below.

Dressing for PI comes in three levels:

- **Casual:** As simple as an open long-sleeve shirt or windbreaker over shorts and T-shirt, plus a bit of barrier lotion. It'll do for a light walk in the forest and most urban ag and landscaping.
- **Serious:** Bushwhacking through PI-ridden woods, or wading into unknown greenery on the job, requires full coverage, serious attention to barrier lotions, and fastidious clean up afterward.
- **Nuclear:** If you're wading in to remove PI, you need hazmat-level armor and battle gear.

The best PI clothing, gloves, and gear are from retailers for workers in outdoor industries. Gempler's and Tractor Supply Company focus on agriculture; Ben Meadows on forestry; Grainger on industry. Home improvement and hardware stores sell cleaners and light gear, with a greater variety usually available through their websites.

Hands

The palms are fairly resistant to urushiol, but the thin skin on the backs of hands is highly susceptible and accessible. I wear gloves even on casual excursions. If you think gloves are clunky, you're not wearing the right type or size. Look for a nifty belt-loop clip to keep your gloves handy. Keep a pair of disposable lightweight nitrile or vinyl gloves on hand in case you need to upgrade on the spot.

- **Casual:** Lightweight gloves such as deer leather, bamboo fabric or synthetics.
- **Serious:** Medium to heavyweight oiled leather gloves, or synthetic or vinyl gloves. Urushiol quickly penetrates latex and rubber gloves. If the leather or fabric gloves become tainted, toss them. The further up the arm the glove goes, the safer you are. Consider wearing disposable lightweight nitrile or vinyl gloves underneath.
- **Nuclear:** Heavyweight nitrile gloves enable grabbing onto the plant.

Arms

A long-sleeved shirt with an undershirt beneath is the key to upper body PI protection. No pullovers — removing them smears urushiol everywhere. Shirts with Velcro or zipper fasteners are handy with gloved hands. Some outdoor shirts are treated to repel insects or block UV rays, and those with mesh vent panels, flaps, and roll up sleeves provide breeziness. In cool weather, avoid scratchy fabrics like rough wool that help urushiol penetrate the skin. Keep your elbows covered. It's easy to back your elbows into plants without notice. Elbow PI is a special kind of gruesome.

> The abbreviation "PI" refers to both poison oak and poison ivy.

Any shirt next to your skin should be made of wicking fabric such as Coolmax, especially in hot weather. The lightweight polyester and cotton blend wicks sweat and moisture away from the body and slows the spread of urushiol via sweat. Favored by athletes and sold in recreation stores

- **Casual:** Wear a lightweight long-sleeved shirt or windbreaker over a T-shirt or tank top.
- **Serious:** Go for medium to heavyweight long-sleeved shirts. Protective oversleeves are good if you prefer short sleeves; at least your elbows are covered. Rubber bands over your cuffs help prevent the glove gap. Wear a barrier lotion underneath for greater protection.
- **Nuclear:** We're talking full-body chemical-resistant coveralls, but they come as

affordable disposables. Lacking that, try a heavyweight canvas jumpsuit or overalls and a thick shirt or canvas jacket, all of it thick enough to greatly slow the urushiol but also washable. Apply barrier lotions beneath.

Legs

Yes, it gets hot and you want to wear shorts. Ever thought about chaps?

- **Casual:** Go for light, loose-fitting canvas pants, or shorts with barrier cream.
- **Serious:** Unlined work dungarees, loose-fitting jeans or heavy canvas pants.
- **Nuclear:** See Nuclear, above.

Feet

The higher up the sock coverage goes, the safer you are, especially in the South and Midwest where poison ivy as a ground vine flourishes, often unseen. Double tie your shoelaces and tuck the ends back into the shoe. Dangling laces are notorious urushiol vectors.

Casual: Sneaky PI amid grass and ground covers is a real risk. So are fallen PI leaves in the autumn. Closed-toed shoes are good; boots are better. If you must do sandals, wear socks and barrier lotion.
Serious: Boots that can be washed off or cleaned with PI solvents.
Nuclear: Vinyl (not rubber) galoshes or other chem-proof footwear.

Head and Neck

You baldies especially should wear hats, but everyone's thin facial and ear skin is extra susceptible to PI. Tie back long hair and ball or braid it. Loose hair can sling urushiol around. Careful with do-rags or head bandanas. It's easy to get PI on the head and a tight sweaty cloth cover ensures your whole scalp gets a rash.

- **Casual:** Barrier lotion on your ears. Seriously. Never leave without it.
- **Serious:** A hat with an all-around brim that protects your PI vulnerable ears is best. Hats meant for sun protection are often perfect, and bucket or fishing hats are good. A baseball cap will do in a pinch and those with a neck shade flap in the back work very well. A loose bandana protects the neck and can be pulled up over the lower face for more coverage. Apply barrier lotion around fabric edges and on all the gaps.
- **Nuclear:** Total coverage with full-face shield and helmet. Or at the very least goggles and outerwear with a tightly closed hood.

Mouth

Mouth masks are often referred to as respirators. Needed when cutting vines (urushiol and aerial roots tend to go flying) and when spraying herbicides.

- **Casual:** Not needed.
- **Serious:** Neck bandana pulled up over the lower face.
- **Nuclear:** Use those rated 99% effective protection from drift by oil-based pesticides. Apply barrier lotion around edges and on all the gaps.

Removing Nuclear Clothes

Once your clothes make serious PI contact, let's call them nuclear. The trick is removing them without spreading urushiol around. If you can, undress outside. Wear gloves for as much as possible, being careful not to let gloves touch bare skin. Disposable nitrile gloves are helpful with this task.

1. Put down a few sheets of newspaper or a kitchen-sized plastic trash bag.
2. Take off shoes (but not socks – very important). Use a bootjack, step or other firm straight surface to pry them off to avoid

touching them with your hands. They're nuclear; set them far aside.

3. Take off over-shirt and lay on newspaper or bag. If you were goofy enough to wear a pullover, slip a large t-shirt over it and then pull them both off.
4. Unzip pants and fold over so the waist is toward the floor. Remove, keeping exterior of pants safely inside. Lay on shirt.
5. Take off headwear such as hat (if washable), bandana, sweatband, and so on, and lay on top.
6. Take off socks and lay on top.
7. Take off under-shirt and lay on top.
8. Loosely fold up clothes.
9. Wrap the newspaper around the bundle, or turn the bag inside out around it.
10. Empty out the whole bundle into the washer.
11. Wad up paper or bag and throw away, do not recycle.
12. Remove gloves and wash your hands.

Better Habits

Outdoors, especially in the woods, there is one primary PI ninja rule: Don't pick your nose. Urushiol is inserted right into your mucous membranes where it goes to town. Touching your eyes with urushiol is awful and can even cause temporary blindness. Getting it in your ears is the most horrible earache ever. At least you can't hear your friends telling you what an idiot you were.

Don't touch your face!

Even if you're wearing gloves, the urushiol can transfer. Don't rub your nose, scratch your chin, wipe your brow, none of it. Stop it. If you must, select a safe place on the inside of your outer shirt and rub with that. Or keep a pocket rag especially for scratching.

Practice safe sweat

Keep something on hand for dabbing off sweat. Wear a wicking-fabric sweatband on hot days or if you perspire easily. An all too typical urushiol path is to get it on your arm and then use your arm to wipe the sweat from your brow. Ultimately, urushiol-laden sweat runs into your eyes — the horrors!

Remember what's behind you

We tend to forget what's behind us — which is why it frequently bites us on the butt. When it's outside our field of vision, we overlook things like backpacks, workbelts, and hats, as well as body parts like elbows and hair. Unseen to us, they're interacting with the outside world — including PI.

Respect the nuclear zone

After being in PI territory, assume anything from your mid-thigh down has urushiol on it. Keep that area away from furniture, vehicle seats and everything else. Beware of kneeling and pressing the PI-ridden back of your lower legs into your rear.

Keep your arms close to the body while walking in the woods

Try not to fling, flail or flop. Bad form. It's also a good way to get spider bit. Don't fondle any plants that you don't know.

Wash your hands *before* going to the bathroom

And after, of course. Sure, you've been aware and haven't encountered any PI. Oh be quiet. Don't take a chance. The price is too great.

Don't use that leaf!

Take folded pocket tissues with you for heaven's sake. Or be darn sure you know that plant well, plus any plant that it may have had contact with it, before you get intimate. You just don't know hell until you've…

Stay away from burning brush piles

Chances are PI is being burnt, too. You definitely don't want to breathe in airborne PI or get the smoke on your skin. It's a certain trip to the doc or even the hospital.

Don't ruin your vacation

PI reconnaissance should be your first act when pitching a tent, renting a cabin, exploring a park, or visiting rural friends. Find out where it's safe for you, and your pet, to go.

Section 7 / Chapter 2

Prevent Secondary Exposure

Chapter Index
- Weird & Tragic Ways We Spread Urushiol Around
- How To Clean Everything

You know how kids can leave sticky yet invisible honey or jelly smudges all over the house? Urushiol [oo-roo-**shee**-ohl] is like that, except it lasts for decades. Most surprise outbreaks of poison oak and ivy (abbreviated in *Itchy Business* as PI) come from exposure to a non-plant source of urushiol. Learn how to trace urushiol vector paths and then clean the heck out of them.

Weird and Tragic Ways We Spread Urushiol Around
- Clothes
- Pets
- Work and Leisure Equipment
- Splattering

Urushiol — the gift that keeps on giving. It barely bonds with most plastic and metal items, so resin micro blobs just sit on top for decades, ready to catch a ride to a new home. Urushiol soaks deeply into cloth, leather, and wood, and close enough contact with those will pass the misery along. You've got to get fastidious, even paranoid, about transferring it around. PI ninja awareness is the key.

Clothes

Outer garments get plenty of PI. In the field, clean your hands after you handle your shoes or shoelaces, the most likely places for residual urushiol. Removing footwear using your bare or socked feet is a good way to get PI between the toes. The apparel you don't see that has the sneakiest PI: backpacks, headwear, and work belts. If you can't run the tainted item through the washing machine, spray or suds it down with a cleaner and rinse it off.

- Spookiest secondary exposure: Wearing the gloves of someone immune to urushiol who handled PI. (They get blasé about their gear.)

Pets

A most likely culprit is the dog or cat that brings urushiol in from outside and rubs against the furniture or you. If your pet encounters PI at a park, it can be spread through your car and then home. Wash pet beds and frequented areas.

Around our nature preserve, after a woods hike all dogs must swim in the pond or be hosed down. Since cats and some dogs don't take kindly to washing, especially when it's cold, keep large pre-moistened PI solvent or waterless-cleaner towelettes around. Or use damp towels, or dry towels with a spray bottle of rubbing alcohol, though dogs hate the smell. Even rolling or romping in tall grass helps remove urushiol from fur.

- Weirdest secondary exposure: PI on your butt and private parts because your urushiol-smeared dog lay on the couch and then you sat down in your underwear.

Work and Leisure Equipment

If it's used outside among plants or rolls through woods and grasslands, there's a good chance it's coated with urushiol. Tires are big-time PI vectors. Don't set objects down in their path. The bottoms of objects make an extra sneaky urushiol-carrying place.

- Grossest secondary exposure: The innards of wildlife that eat PI berries and leaves.

Splattering

For spewing urushiol all over your face, hands, clothes and surroundings, nothing beats the efficiency of wee-deaters, trimmers, and lawnmowers. Motorized cutters expel PI for an amazingly far distance. ATV and tractor grass-cutters operated on rural lots, farms, and ranches are notorious urushiol-dispensing machines. Machetes, scythes, and another chopping tools also splatter urushiol. Cut PI cleanly with hand loppers, nothing mechanized. More in the Eradicating the Plant section.

If you christen the world with urushiol in one of these ways, wash the area down. If unable, mark the area with danger flags and pray for rain.

- Most tragic secondary exposure: Outdoor festivals held at freshly mown sites that had PI hidden in the grass.

How To Clean Everything

- Tools and Tips for Cleaning
- Cleaning in the Washing Machine
- Cleaning by Hand
- Inside Home, Office or Workroom
- Choose Your Cleaner

Here's a typical scenario. Urushiol is on the heel of your shoes. You put your shoes — and urushiol — on the stool or coffee table, then touch it and later — eeek! — your nose or eyes. The key is to retrace that urushiol vector. Don't forget to include your vehicle and outdoor gathering areas.

Tools and Tips for Cleaning

Make sure you're well covered when you clean up urushiol, and wash any exposed skin frequently during the process.

It's best to wear vinyl or nitrile gloves while cleaning; don't choose latex or rubber. Use non-absorbent plastic net scrubbers and brushes. Rags risk flinging urushiol about, and regular cellulose sponges are difficult to rinse thoroughly or wash in machines.

For information on PI in the news and updates on products, please visit the book website:
WWW.ITCHY.BIZ

Cleaning in the Washing Machine

If you can launder the clothes or item in a washing machine, it'll get a thorough cleaning.

- Empty material into the washer.
- Use high-surfactant laundry detergent with borax, washing soda, bleach or oxygen bleach.
- If the item is especially nuclear, add PI solvent.
- Set the water level to high. Select extra rinse if you have that option.
- Wash twice in warm to hot water.
- Then do a wash cycle with just detergent to clean the machine.

Cleaning by Hand

Keep a tall tub or trashcan of detergent water with a scrub brush on hand for dunking tools, and a rinse tub as well. Keep the item immersed during scrubbing to prevent urushiol from splattering. Switch out detergent water frequently and dispose of carefully.

If the object is unable to immerse, suds it up with a sponge or spray it down with a cleaner. Rinse the object off with a steady flow of water, being careful to aim downward and not splash urushiol about.

Inside Home, Office or Workroom

Once inside, urushiol vectors are frequently touched objects:

- Toilet handles and seats (ow!)
- Door and cabinet knobs
- Faucets and sink objects

Clean all furniture and counters accessed right after you come inside or where you first sit down. Clean, clean, and clean some more.

> Items listed are not endorsements, but used only to demonstrate the types of products available.

Choose Your Cleaner

Match the cleaner to the amount of urushiol exposure. They range from strong dishwashing detergents such as Dawn, to cleaners for mopping floors, to liquid citrus or pine oil cleaners, to industrial cleaners.

Waterless cleaners like Goop make it easy to clean in the field. Coat the item with Goop and wipe it off. If it's very urushiol tainted or has lots of small places for urushiol to hide, get after it with a PI solvent. Pre-moistened large towelettes are good for this. Wash afterward with high-surfactant soap and rinse with lots of clean water. Use 90% rubbing alcohol on small, non-durable items.

CLEANERS & FLOOR CLEANERS

Citra Solv Cleaner/Degreaser by Citra Solv
- The power of orange-peel solvents and surfactants.

Pine Sol
- The power of pine tar solvents and surfactants.

Simple Green
- Adheres to Green Seal eco-standards.

DISHWASHING DETERGENTS

Ultra Dishwashing Liquid or **Direct Dishwashing Foam Pump** by Dawn
- Super powerful, yet safe enough to use on oil-covered seabirds.

Ultra Oxy Plus Power Degreaser by Palmolive
- A serious contender.

GLOVES

Nitrile Disposable Gloves by Mr. Clean
- Stands up to strong chemicals.

Vinyl Disposable Gloves by Mr. Clean
- Stands up to many chemicals.

LAUNDRY DETERGENTS

Laundry Detergent, Free by Arm & Hammer
- Laundry soda power.

Liquid Laundry Detergent, Perfume & Dye Free by OxiClean
- Oxygen power.

LAUNDRY ADDITIVES

Borax Natural Laundry Booster by 20 Mule Team
- A salt of boric acid, tough stuff.

Oxygen Bleach Plus by biokleen
- Hydrogen peroxide and sodium carbonate zinged by grapefruit seed extract and softened by glycerin.

Super Wash Soda by Arm & Hammer
- Sodium Carbonate detergent booster.

Versatile Stain Remover, Free or **Baby Stain Soaker** by OxiClean
- The household oxygen pioneer, sodium carbonate and sodium percarbonate powder in water is used to create a high-oxygen solution. These versions are additive free.

PI SOLVENTS

Ivy X Post-Contact Skin Cleanser by CoreTex
- A strong solvent-surfactant combo with chamomile, calendula, green tea, and white oak extracts for skin healing. Comes in a variety of sizes and formats. Available online and at most agricultural and outdoor stores, often sold directly to outdoor industries.

Tecnu Outdoor Skin Cleanser by Tec Labs
- The best-selling PI solvent-surfactant combo is well loved and rightly so. It rocks, a lifesaver for many people. Available online and at most drug, agricultural and outdoor stores. Comes in a variety of sizes and formats.

SCRUBBERS

Dobie All-Purpose Pads by Scotch-Brite
- Like a sponge, but non-absorbent polyester net.

Heavy Duty Scouring Pads by Scotch Brite
- Scrubber fabric often found on top of sponges, but sans sponge.

Innovative Dish Washing Net Cloth by Top Clean
- Net pieces 11 inches square, cut to desired size

WATERLESS CLEANERS

Goop Hand Cleaner, Orange
- Thick cream long favored by mechanics to remove grease. The more recent Orange Goop is a lightweight gel with a nice smell. Available in several formats, including pre-moistened towels that are very handy for wiping down dogs and tools.

Eradicating the Plant

Section Index
1. Planning and Preparation
2. Bye, Bye, PI

Should it stay or should it go? Seems like a no brainer when it comes to poison oak or ivy (abbreviated in *Itchy Business* as PI). Yet it's not. Sometimes the PI infestation is so huge that it's most feasible to manage it. Other times wildlife or erosion concerns mean it's best left alone. Learn in this section learn how to evaluate the situation and make a PI plan, suit up for PI removal or management, and replace PI with something preferable.

Section 8 / Chapter 1
Prepare for Battle

Chapter Index
- Leave, Reduce or Eradicate?
- The Itchy Business 5-Step Plan
- Marking PI Patches
- Timing: Seasonal Cycles
- Timing: Lunar Cycles
- Safety Gear

PI is one persistent plant. Just like dealing with the rash, PI ninja patience is the key. Spray, cut or mulch it once or twice and it's bound to come back. Especially where it grows strongly with plenty of water and a few hours of direct sunlight each day.

Leave, Reduce or Eradicate?

There are three choices when it comes to PI:
- **Leave it**, but mark prominently with warning tape.
- **Reduce it**, by containing its growth and preventing berry production.
- **Eradicate it**, and establish stronger, more beneficial plants in the location.

On our nature preserve, we do all three. We keep it PI free around home and work buildings and restrict it for another 20 yards or so. Most trails and roads are flanked by a yard-wide PI-free zone. We also cut monster vines that threaten the health of a tree or are spewing PI berries over pathways. Other than that we let it be.

Contemplate the costs of eradication. Herbicides and their dispensing equipment can add up. You must budget for multiple eradication campaigns over a couple years to truly halt the plant. Manual removal is cheaper (unless you pay a service or hire goats to do it), but is it worth risking a major rash? Even keeping PI reduced is an annual endeavor and in some places more often.

> The abbreviation "PI" refers to both poison oak and poison ivy.

Consider other costs as well. Will taking out PI destroy adjacent beneficial plants? Even a slight drift of systemic glyphosate herbicides can spell doom for pond and creek inhabitants. Are there birds or animals that depend on the plant for food? Large tree vines provide nesting for birds and even raccoons. Its sprawling root and rhizome system stalls erosion.

If it simply has to go, whether it's a backyard vine that your dog loves to rub against, or a monster shrub that is eating your barn, let's do this thing! The same techniques work if you just want to restrain its domain. You can go manual or use herbicides. Usually it's a combination. Even if you're a fan of chemmies, a first cut is almost always needed.

The Itchy Business 5-Step Plan

Follow the Itchy Business 5-step plan for success. Allow at least two years for the PI eradication process, even a light patch.

1. Cut down as much of the plant as possible.
2. Prune or apply herbicides to regrowth.
3. Grub out the roots and rhizomes.
4. Bake the hell out of it.
5. Overseed the area.

An optimal PI eradication schedule goes like this:

1st year: late spring — 3rd and 4th lunar quarter
- Prune when the plant is flowering or setting

berries.
- Mark areas for follow up.

1st year: summer — 3rd and 4th lunar quarter
- Prune and apply herbicides on regrowth.

1st year: early fall — 3rd and 4th lunar quarter
- Final opportunity to apply herbicides.

1st year: late fall through winter — 4th lunar quarter
- Grub roots.

2nd year: spring — 3rd and 4th lunar quarter
- Check for regrowth.
- Prune and apply herbicides.

2nd year: summer
- Mulch heavily. Maintain through winter.

2nd year: spring
- Check for regrowth. Treat as needed.

2nd year: spring to early summer — 1st and 2nd lunar quarter, New and Full Moons
- Overseed with preferred greenery.

Marking PI Patches

Marking for PI on our nature preserve is year round for us. Places where PI tends to spring back along the roads and trails are marked, as are other places where it's being eradicated or managed, plus off-trail areas with PI that might tempt hikers.

Vinyl flagging tape in hot pink grabs attention since it's such an odd color to see outdoors and the pink-PI alliteration helps people remember. The tape lasts a year or two, shorter if in bright sunlight or extreme heat and wind. Biodegradable tapes are available, but who wants to keep wading into the PI to replace them?

Sometimes the only place to mark PI is on the plant itself, so have nitrile gloves around for the task. The tape can be also tied to stakes or dowels. Mark a sprawling area of PI ground vines with construction flags, very helpful when you have a tree with a 360-degree PI zone.

Be sure to mark areas where you are trying to eradicate PI. Though the leaves may be gone, the toxic roots remain, now lacking foliage to alert their presence. If eradicating the plant in a public area, it's wise to create warning signs stating: "Poison ivy [or oak] removal in process. Do not enter or tamper with soil."

Flagging Tape by Gemplers
- Comes in standard, plus fluorescent, striped, and polka dot when it needs to stand out. Biodegradable also available.

Stake Pattern Flag by Gemplers
- A diagonal stripe pattern on a 4"x5" flag and 30" stake wire for greater visibility.

Timing: Seasonal Cycles

To successfully eradicate or contain PI you must accommodate the plant's growing cycles and work with seasonal and lunar fluctuations, PI ninja style.

Spring means the PI is surging with plant power. Pruning just encourages it and applying herbicides barely makes a dent. Mark your PI patches and wait.

In late spring and early summer, PI is in flower and setting berries. Plant energy is focused on reproduction. It's the perfect time to prune and apply herbicides.

Summer is so hot in the South and Southwest that plant growth slows, making it a poor time to apply synthetic systemic herbicides, but perfect for spraying natural contact herbicides.

In early fall before color changes occur is another optimal time to apply herbicides. The plant takes in a hearty shot, but there is little leaf regrowth.

Winter is the prime time for pruning and grubbing. The foliage isn't in your face, but the stems and roots are toxic as ever.

> Items listed are not endorsements, but used only to demonstrate the types of products available.

Timing: Lunar Cycles

Gardening by Moon phases has centuries of anecdotal evidence. Many animal species mate or spawn at Full and New Moons, so plant reproduction could sync up as well.

1st and 2nd Lunar Quarters: Waxing

At the New Moon, the Sun and Moon are conjunct. Tides are at their highest. For the following two weeks the Moon waxes and increases in brightness. The plant emphasizes moving energy into leaves and stems above the ground, as if responding to the waxing light.

According to Moon gardening, this is a bad time for pruning to restrain regrowth since plants tend to spring back with vigor. Nor is a good time to spray systemic herbicides since they must be rapidly absorbed into the roots to be effective. However, seeding is optimal.

3rd and 4th Lunar Quarters: waning

At the Full Moon, the Sun and Moon are opposite each other in the sky. Tides are once again at their highest. Over the following two weeks, the Moon wanes and becomes less visible in the sky. Plants respond by emphasizing their roots.

According to Moon gardening, this is the optimal time to prune for decreased plant regrowth, and to spray herbicides which must be absorbed into the roots to be effective. In the mid to late 4th quarter, the hold of roots in the ground become less tenacious, making it a good time to grub them out.

New and Full Moons

New and Full Moon phases last three days, though usually only the middle date is marked on the calendar. These are optimal times to sow seeds and prune for encouraging regrowth.

Quarter Moons

A second Moon gardening camp maintains that plants are solely in sync with tidal patterns. Tides are highest at New and Full Moons and lowest mid-way between. They assert there is less regrowth if you prune at the quarter Moon phases which occur at beginning of the 2nd and 4th quarters.

Merging the two lunar camps, the beginning of the 4th quarter is the absolute most perfect time for pruning PI to restrain regrowth.

Safety Gear

Consider that a teeny nick of a PI leaf releases enough urushiol [oo-roo-**shee**-ohl] to give hundreds of sensitive people a rash. Now think about what cutting the stem or vine in two will do. They are loaded with large resin canals that feed urushiol-laden sap to smaller canals in the leaves. It flows out in torrents. Fools used to collect this stuff to use as permanent ink.

Before embarking on your eradication quest, serious safety gear is required. Visit the Defending Yourself section and follow the advice in Prevent Skin Contact, focusing on the Nuclear level instructions.

If you'll be using a vehicle, pack at least two 5-gallon containers of detergent water with tight lids. Ideal are those with a spigot. Use one for cleaning and the other for dipping tainted tools. If that's not possible, bring disposable towels of industrial waterless cleaners. Keep some cardboard boxes on hand to contain tainted tools.

Also bring a good-sized jar of cotton balls or rags soaked in rubbing alcohol, plus plenty of PI solvent. If you're going backwoods, don't forget the to-go packets of PI solvent. Bring cleaning wipes for the dog if it's coming along.

After working with PI, follow the advice in Cleaning Off Urushiol, located in the Understanding Urushiol section. Remember to wash the tools thoroughly when you return and clean the buckets, too.

Section 8 / Chapter 2

Bye, Bye, PI

Chapter Index
- Cut it Down, Grub it Out
- Herbicide 101
- Herbicide Equipment
- Synthetic Herbicides
- Synthetic Herbicide Application 101
- Natural Herbicides
- Natural Herbicide Blends
- Vine, Shrub, and Tree Stumps
- The Final Bake
- Cleanup
- Paid Services and Goats
- Overseeding

The removal of poison oak or ivy (abbreviated in *Itchy Business* as PI) is a war of attrition. Keep cutting, chopping, grubbing, applying herbicides, and smothering with mulch until roots and rhizomes use up all their stored energy and can no longer send up new growth. In shady places, they don't have a lot of reserves and are easier to kill. Sunny plots of PI can be an extreme challenge, especially those with roots extending beneath structures or pavement. Plan on PI scouting missions every few months to deal with regrowth.

Cut it Down, Grub it Out
- Stems and Vines
- Roots and Rhizomes
- Diffuse or Gigantic Patches

Using a weedeater or other motorized cutter to remove PI will result in spraying everything, including your body, with urushiol [oo-roo-**shee**-ohl]. In most cases there is no choice but to get up and personal when exterminating the plant.

PI does not go gently into that good night. It fights back. If you cut PI on a hot day, urushiol can squirt out. Egad! Stems can be springy, slapping back at you, especially eastern poison ivy. Jiggling a PI vine to cut it can cause a rain of berries and leaves to shower upon you. If circumstances allow, consider doing the first cut with goats.

Stems and Vines

Nothing beats a lopper for PI pruning in most cases. The cut is clean. Bury me with my Fiskars 21" lopper. I love that thing.

There are two approaches to lopper technology:

Anvil: A flat blade chops against a flat surface.
- Best for: Dry or dead stems and vines.

The author's Fiskars PowerGear® lopper.

Bypass: Two curved metal blades slide past each other like scissors.
- Best for: Supple live stems and vines. Can open wide and cut sizable diameters. Must be able to get the lopper around the entire diameter, not always possible with attached vines.

If you're doing a lot of work, or lack upper-body strength, pay more for those with gearing and ratchet technology that enable easier cutting. Metal quality increases the price. There are even titanium loppers!

Loppers come in three styles:

Hand pruners: Under 12" for close-in work on small stems and vines.

100

Long-handled loppers: Capable of cutting stems and vines up to 2" in diameter, sometimes bigger. These range from 14" to 28" or more in length, with 21" to 24" being easiest for most people to handle. It can be a struggle to execute big cuts with longer loppers, making the user more likely to land face down in the PI.

Fiskars Pruning Stik® lopper at 5' fills the gap between long-handled loppers and telescopic loppers.

Telescopic loppers: Lopper blades are attached to a 6' to 10' pole. Handy for cutting small to moderate PI at a distance, especially reaching through a sprawl of PI to cut the mother vine.

When it comes to monster eastern poison ivy and western poison oak vines ascending a tree, rock or structure, sometimes there's no way to get a lopper around it. Axes work great for this. Be aware that dry aerial roots go flying out like cat dander. Make sure you wear a respiratory mask rated for oily particulates, not just the usual dust mask. More details below in Vine, Shrub, and Tree Stumps.

Roots and Rhizomes

GRUBBING

A PI ninja master learns to perceive the patterns of PI roots, rhizomes, and ground vines. Older ones usually have wider diameters. Trace them to the mother plant. Sometimes it's obvious. An eastern poison ivy vine growing up a tree will send out a 360-degree pattern like spokes on a wheel. Other times, roots might be coming from under pavement or structures. In the Identifying the Plant section, The American Axis of Itching chapter will help you discover the PI species native to your area, and then learn its growing habits in the Know Your Adversary chapter.

Grubbing, or pulling out roots and rhizomes, is much easier when the soil is damp. Even better, do it just before a rain so that the torrents of released urushiol wash safely into the soil. Best done in fall and winter after leaf fall.

Roots and rhizomes are usually 1" to 3" deep. Prepare them for grubbing by lifting and loosening with a tool. Listen for the connections of descending feeder roots to pop. If they're well rooted, chances are you're getting closer to the mother plant. A bow rake with hard tines or a 3-tine cultivator hoe work well. A 2-prong weeder hoe includes a blade for chopping. A pointed hoe will do, but in dense clays it's harder to slip under roots and rhizomes. Deeper ones may need some digging or hoeing.

To grub, stand with your knees slightly bent for stability. Start at the edge or weakest point. Go along the root or rhizome and pull directly up. Since urushiol-laden debris will be shooting upward, cover your mouth and nose with a mask or bandana. PI up the nose makes you look like Rudolph for weeks.

CHOPPING

Sometimes grubbing is not possible or can only be partially done. Chop the PI roots and rhizomes into pieces 10" or under. This technique, used to control bamboo, turns the energy of one strong root into many smaller weaker ones. When the PI re-grows, it will be much more manageable and easier to kill.

Use a straight-blade hoe, also called a chopper, scraper, or square edge root cutter. A sharpshooter shovel will also work and keep your foot further from the root. Maintain sharp edges for easier chopping.

BOILING WATER AND FLAME WEEDERS

Don't. PI roots may hate heat, but inhaling vaporized urushiol — it attaches to particles such as soot and water impurities — will surely send you to the hospital.

Diffuse or Gigantic Patches

With diffuse PI in fields, all you can do is mow. It goes all sneaky bonsai, but at least doesn't replicate. Mow before rains when possible.

If you have bucks to burn and a towering PI monster or a field of shrubs, hire a top-down mulcher. Like a giant lawnmower on a swing arm, it presses down over the plant and chews it into a pile of shred that should be handled like it's uranium. Do this only in winter.

Herbicide 101

Herbicides work on plants or seeds:
- Pre-emergent: prevents seeds from sprouting, applied as granules
- Post-emergent: kills live plants

PI herbicides come in two methods:
- Foliar: destroys plant matter on contact
- Systemic: kills after being absorbed and circulated through the plant

And they come in two styles:
- Synthetic: made from petrochemicals
- Natural: based on horticultural vinegar or refined plant oils

Herbicides work best on tender foliage. Spring seems like an ideal time, but there's often not enough leaf matter. More leaf surface area enables more herbicide to get where it needs to go. The optimum process is to cut back the plant in spring and apply herbicides to bushy regrowth a few weeks later. For every inch of trunk or vine that's cut, allow a foot of regrowth before herbicides.

Herbicide Equipment

The goal is to get the least amount of herbicide needed onto the leaves. Anything else is inefficient and wasteful. PI ninjas don't do that. Highly precise wicking applicators that paint herbicide onto leaves now join traditional spray rigs.

> Items listed are not endorsements, but used only to demonstrate the types of products available.

Wicking Applicators

A reservoir handle 36" or more long contains herbicide that is gravity fed into an applicator. Some are capped with a 2" brush or sponge. Others look like hockey sticks with an 8" wide sponge or rope applicator.

Best thing about wicking applicators is no herbicide drift. A longtime technology in agriculture and large-scale landscaping, it's relatively new on the consumer level. Kinks in keeping the wick saturated without dripping are still being worked out. The more expensive units get better consumer reviews.

Wicking applicators can be towed behind ATVs. Since PI control is targeted, rather than broadcast, they require a two-person crew: one to drive and another to monitor the applicator.

Red Weeder by Smucker
- 10" sponge at end of 36" wand. Leaky, best for natural herbicides.

Weed Thief by Sideswipe
- 10" wick rope at end of 36" wand. Top cover enables reaching PI under other plants.

Weeding Brush by Hudson
- 2" brush at end of 38" wand. Precise.

Spray Rigs

The tank of an herbicide sprayer is pumped or pressurized to force out a spray. Most common are 1-gallon tanks that must be set down and pumped periodically by hand, making the air pressure created erratic and uneven. Cute half-gallon hand-held versions are easier to keep constant.

Truly rockin' are 4-gallon tanks mounted on backpacks and pumped as you go along using a piston-powered lever. It allows a PI ninja to monitor the piston sound and pump precisely to create the perfect pressure for every situation.

A higher pressure will reach further. Medium pressure facilitates a quick, targeted burst to hit specific plants.

Be sure the nozzle is adjustable from a fine wide spray for covering large areas, to a narrow stream for small places. If you've never sprayed before, fill the tank with water and practice first.

If you have a bonkers amount of PI that needs eradication and covers a large area, large tank versions can be mounted on ATVs. Since PI control is targeted, rather than broadcast, they require a two-person crew: one to drive and another to spray.

Synthetic Herbicides

Most widely used of the systemic pack are glyphosates (aka Roundup, Eraser) that kill by inhibiting plant synthesis of certain vital amino acids. But PI is a woody plant and requires the addition of a brush killer, usually triclorpyl, a triethylamine salt.

The pros and cons of systemic glyphosate herbicides are hotly debated. They're easy to use, concentrated, and portable, which is a huge benefit in the field. If they reach the roots the plant is thoroughly killed. Compared to the caustic contact herbicides of yore, they're a significant piece of bio-engineering. If used briefly and infrequently, and with proper safety practices, they're safe to humans. If applied judiciously and minimally, and with proper safety practices, they're safe for the environment.

"If" is a mighty big word for being two letters. Research teams from World Health Organization have cited glyphosate as a probable carcinogen. Studies in Sweden have linked glyphosate herbicides to non-Hodgkin lymphoma. Statistics from the nation of Columbia show a high incidence of birth defects and cancers near where they're sprayed. PubMed database is full of studies that provoke grave concern. EPA is investigating the impact of glyphosate herbicides on aquatic creatures. As glyphosate breaks down, one byproduct, formaldehyde, is very toxic to fish and amphibians. Sometimes the problem is not glyphosate but added chemicals that help herbicides penetrate the plant.

As with everything in *Itchy Business*, be a PI ninja. More is not better. Use glyphosate herbicides accurately and stingily. Save money while being easier on yourself and the environment. More on how to do that in Synthetic Herbicide Application 101, below.

Roundup Poison Ivy Plus Tough Brush Killer by Monsanto
- Comes in a ready-to-use spray bottle or mix-it-yourself concentrate. 1% glyphosate & 0.1% triclopyr

Synthetic Herbicide Application 101

Make a little go a long way with PI ninja philosophy. It is all about smartness and precision.

Any glyphosate herbicide that reaches the ground is wasted. It breaks down more slowly in soil and washes into aquatic ecosystems where it can inflict damage. Spray using as fine a mist as possible, but be aware that smaller droplets drift more. Be careful with drips from wicking applicators.

The weather should be between 60 to 90 degrees for maximum assimilation by the plant. If there's complete cloud cover, the uptake rate may be too slow. If it's too sunny and hot, the herbicide may evaporate before being absorbed.

Wind speed must be 5 mph or less for spraying. Don't guess. Check a weather website or better yet carry a wind-speed reader.

Keep all synthetic herbicide sprays at least 30 yards away from waterways. Be very careful with drift around bodies of water. Wicking applicators can get much closer. Avoid spraying during wildlife breeding seasons and around nesting areas.

Systemic herbicides take time to set before rain or foot traffic, from 30 minutes to 6 hours depending on the brand. Keep non-hoofed animals and bare-footed people off treated areas for several hours.

Natural Herbicides

- Orange and Other Oils
- Horticultural Vinegar and Other Acids
- Salt
- Soap

Most natural herbicides are contact herbicides that kill in a simple and direct way. Spray on the plant, watch it wither. Whatever it touches it kills. Problem is, it doesn't reach the roots and PI is a plant with extensive roots.

Contact herbicides work by dessication: dry the plant chemically until it's dead dead dead. Pucker that sucker. Burn baby burn. They work quickly. Spraying in full sunlight on a hot day can kill a susceptible plant in a few hours. Unlike glyphosate systemics, they can work in as low as 40 degrees. With natural herbicides, count on spraying to treat PI regrowth for several years. Hold on to the hope that the plant eventually weakens and succumbs.

Natural herbicides rely on caustic substances like horticultural vinegar, super-potent soap, or concentrated oils that are derived from oranges, plus cloves and rosemary. All strip away the plant's protective waxy exterior cuticle, sending dehydration into overdrive. They wreak havoc with membranes of interior plant cells, so they leak, too. Flat out devastation.

Natural contact herbicides are far safer for humans and other living creatures than synthetics. But overuse of horticultural vinegar and plant oils can kill earthworms and strip soil of microorganisms that keep it healthy. Salt can render soil useless. Vinegar will turn soil very slightly more acidic.

Orange and Other Oils

Oils extracted and refined from the peels of oranges and other citrus fruit are so potent they act like solvents. Referred to as orange oil, the active ingredient is d-Limonene. Look for brands with a significant percentage.

Orange oil is highly concentrated and fabulously portable, non-toxic and quickly biodegradable. And it smells purdy. Being oily, it sticks better to plant leaves than horticultural vinegar. Orange oil paired with an emulsifier stays evenly mixed with water and doesn't junk up spray nozzles.

Eugenol is extracted from clove oil. A feature of many natural herbicides, it is not widely available by itself. Rosemary oil is also used.

Horticultural Vinegar & Other Acids

Horticultural vinegar is rough stuff made by fermenting wood. It comes in a 10% to 20% concentration of acetic acid. That's two to four times stronger than the vinegar used on your salad or pickles.

Horticultural vinegar is applied full strength or slightly diluted. It is sometimes blended with other compounds; see below. Even concentrated, it's bulky to use. And what a stink.

Don't get casual about it because it's called vinegar. It is acetic acid. Treat it with caution as you would muratic acid or any other caustic substance. Wear nitrile glove and safety goggles, especially when mixing, and stand back from any vapors. Acetic acid can irritate and even burn skin, eyes, respiratory and digestive systems.

Citric acid is featured in some natural herbicides and is usually derived from fermentation of special sugar solutions.

Salt

Salt works as a desiccant by sucking moisture out of plant foliage. Recommended only if used sparingly and there are no plans to grow in the area for over a year. Salt can accumulate in the soil and cause long-term problems, even impacting plants a significant distance away. Salt is bad news in well water and aquifers.

For information on PI in the news and updates on products, please visit the book website:

WWW.ITCHY.BIZ

Soap

Soap also helps erode the plant's exterior cuticle, especially potent insecticidal soaps. But they're not potent enough for PI. In herbicides based on vinegar and plant oils, a milder dishwashing detergent is included to act as a surfactant that breaks water surface tension and helps herbicides cling to leaf surfaces.

Natural Herbicide Blends

An effective natural herbicide for a brushy well-rooted plant like PI must be far stronger than for your usual weeds.

Vinegar Only
- Horticultural vinegar   1 gallon
- Soap   1 tablespoon

Orange Oil Only
- Water   1 gallon
- Orange oil   1 cup
- Soap   1 teaspoon

Vinegar and Orange Oil
- Horticultural vinegar 1 gallon
- Orange oil   ¼ cup
- Soap   1 tablespoon

Vinegar, Orange Oil, and Salt
- Horticultural vinegar 1 gallon
- Orange oil   1 tablespoon
- Soap   1 tablespoon
- Salt   ¼ cup

Several commercially prepared natural herbicides are available that work optimally in sprayers and cling well to plant leaves. Use as strong a solution as possible.

Avenger Organic Weed Killer by Avenger
- Emulsified orange oil with additives to help adherence to plant leaves. Potent stuff! 17.5% d-Limonene.

Burnout by Bonide
- Emulsified eugenol from clove oil plus citric acid, with additives to help adherence to plant leaves. 8.0% eugenol.

Weed & Grass Killer by EcoSMART
- Emulsified eugenol from clove oil with additives to help adherence to plant leaves. 5.0% eugenol.

Vine, Shrub, and Tree Stumps

For larger established vines, shrubs or trees, cut a few inches above the ground. Cut an X across the exposed surface so the herbicide or decomposer can penetrate. To prevent vines from growing back together, make an additional cut a few inches above the first to create a gap.

Synthetic Systemic Herbicides

Immediately treat the fresh-cut stump with triclopyr. Look for versions with squeeze or paintbrush applicators. Triclopyr takes months to biodegrade to benign levels and breakdown byproducts persist even longer. Use miserly and with great caution.

Cutting large PI stems creates an eternal urushiol fountain of hurt. After the herbicide is absorbed, cover the exposed surface with any kind of paint or a horticultural wound product.

Organic Decomposition

Hasten the rotting of PI stumps by pouring molasses or a thick sugar solution on them. Cheap horticultural molasses is available, but you can even use old jams, honey, and so on. The sugar encourages microbes to multiply and gorge on the wood. Keep stumps moist and re-apply sugar as needed. Do not use compost facilitators as they may encourage PI sprouts.

Cut Vine & Stump Killer by Ferti-Lome
- 8.8% triclopyr.

Poison Ivy and Tough Brush Killer by Ortho
- 8.0% triclopyr.

Tree Wound Dressing by Treekote
- Black asphalt emulsion that sticks to plant surfaces. Look for bottles with applicator tops. Coat exposed area thoroughly.

The Final Bake

Once you've pummeled the PI into submission, it's time for the coup de grâce. PI roots and rhizomes hate extended periods of high temperatures. Both techniques work best with summer heat and lots of sunlight.

Mulch

Make what little life is left in the roots and rhizomes cry uncle by rotting them with moist heat. Mulch the area with no less than a 6" layer of mulch. Pile mulch over cut and treated stumps. Use fine-textured mulches that decompose quickly. Sawdust works great. Do not use compost. You want the heat of decomposition to do its wonders. Keep adding mulch as it decomposes to maintain height. Give it a year to work. This also prepares the area for overseeding.

Soil Oven

To clear a large area of PI and every other living plant, use 2 to 4 mil. plastic tarps to create a soil oven. It can be effective as soon as 2 months in full sunlight or take many times longer in shady areas. It works best if the soil stays moist.

Cut the PI as close to the ground as feasible or pre-treat with herbicides. Minimize the air space between ground and tarp to maximize the heat. A second tarp will boost the heat level, especially if there is an inch or more gap between the two. The edges will be cooler, so extend the plastic a foot past the PI patch. It works best if you dig trenches and bury the tarp ends in the soil. If that's not possible, weight the edges down as thoroughly as possible.

If the PI plot is sunny, clear plastic works great. A semi-shady location needs to collect heat, so use black plastic. Leave on months longer than would be required for herbaceous weeds. You do end up with huge sheets of urushiol-covered plastic. Do not recycle.

Clean Up

Remember that dead PI is just as nasty as live PI. Do not leave roots, rhizomes, and other PI parts about to become urushiol landmines. Bag them up in 3 mil. thick contractor garbage bags and dispose. Beware of bag bottoms being covered in urushiol from sitting on PI ground. If you must leave PI debris, pile it up, stack brush on top, and mark the spot with pink flagging tape, or bury it deep.

Paid Services

Livestock

Goats are known for finding PI to be tasty, high-protein stuff, especially in the spring. They eat it down to nub, even consume vines. Keep in mind they will eat everything and poop everywhere. You must mark the patch and expect regrowth. Best used as either regular maintenance or as a step 1 in the Itchy Business 5-Step Plan.

Services

Many landscape services will remove PI and charge you a high dollar for it, too. You'll still need to monitor for regrowth. Make sure you hose everything down afterward or have it done just prior to a rain.

Overseeding

Once PI has been throttled to an apparent death, something needs to take its place and thwart regrowth. Cover plants also keep unsuspecting folks from digging around. Since it's impossible to grub out 100% of the toxic PI roots, seeds are the best option.

Native plants have a good chance of being vigorous enough to override PI. Tough prairie grasses with wildflowers are a good choice if sunlight allows. Sea oats and prairie rye are good for shade. For help selecting the right seeds, contact your local Native Plant Society or naturalist organization. Many nature centers have native plant displays.

PI Reader

Section Index
1. Strange Facts and Terrible Tales
2. Debunking the Bull Manure

Wrapping up the wonderful world of poison oak and ivy (abbreviated in Itchy Business as PI) is a compendium of non-essential information that will make you the conversational hit of any party. Who else will bring up self-mummification through urushiol [oo-roo-shee-ohl] tea? People have all kinds of crazy ideas about PI. Read on to learn pithy replies for effective and funny mythbusting.

Section 9 / Chapter 1

Strange Facts and Terrible Tales

Chapter Index
- Japan: Dangerous Beauty and Mummified Monks
- Urushiol Around the Globe
- Cashews, Mangos, and Toxic Treats
- Poison Ivy and Europe
- Poison Ivy in Other Languages
- Native Americans, PI Masters — Not
- Poison Oak as Art
- Pop Culture Poison Ivy
- Poison Ivy, Batman's Nemesis

Discover where eastern poison ivy (*Toxicodendron radicans*) exists in surprising pockets in Europe, thanks to crazed traveling botanists. Meet the weirdos here at home who've turned PI into art and pop culture, from peppy '50s songs to comic books where she reigns as a misunderstood supervillain. Learn about relatives of PI that spread their not-quite-as-toxic love over much of the planet.

Japan: Dangerous Beauty and Mummified Monks

PI has plenty of *Toxicodendron* cousins back home in East Asia, where *Toxicodendron radicans* first arose and still thrives. The entire genre division called *Venenata* is composed of urushiol-laden trees, the largest of all *Toxicodendrons*. Everything's big about them. A leaf consists of 7 to 13 six-inch leaves arranged in pairs along on stem. The flower stems are six inches or more and — horrors! — they can fume urushiol.

> The abbreviation "PI" refers to both poison oak and poison ivy.

As cousins go, they're badass. Imagine a tree over 60 feet tall dripping with urushiol. That's the Japanese lacquer or varnish tree, *Toxicodendron vernicifluum*, which also grows in northern China. The lacquer refined from its urushiol-laden sap is called *urushi* (漆), giving urushiol its name.

Family guilds of craftsmen who tap and refine the sap develop immunity to urushiol over generations. And also to the sap's foul smell, one assumes. There is a special class of artists who specialize in *urushi-e* (漆絵) or lacquer picture. The amount of urushiol in these exquisite artworks makes you itch just to gaze upon them. And they're so damn dangerous. How very Japanese.

Naturally a brownish-black sap, the *urushi* is tinted with oxides to create black and red lacquers that are hypnotically deep and able to retain their color forever. They're super shiny because urushi polymerizes as it dries, making them extremely durable and a tad less toxic. Beyond *urushi-e*, the lacquer is used in Japanese tableware, musical instruments, archery bows, and small fine objects like fountain pens and jewelry where durability is prized. Is better to look good than to feel good, yes?

Those unlucky saps that don't develop immunity (see what I did there?) are prey to *urushi-kabure*, or lacquer poisoning by exposure to fumes. German geographer Johannes Justus Rein described his experience studying the art:

> "It appears in a mild reddening and swelling of the back of the hands, the face, eyelids, ears, the region of the navel and lower parts of the body, especially the scrotum. In all these parts, great heat is felt and violent itching and burning, causing many sleepless nights. In two or three days, the crisis is reached, and the swelling immediately subsides. In severe cases, small festering boils form also."

A byproduct of *urushi* production is Japan wax. Temple caretakers love how candles made from it burn with a smokeless flame that doesn't smudge sacred artworks. Japan wax candles also smell like something only a mother could love. Hooray for incense!

Then it gets weird, really weird. Between the 11th and 19th century, extremely austere monks from the Japanese Vajrayana school of Buddhism practiced *Sokushinbutsu* — the art of self-mummification. For a decade, a monk would exercise and restrict his diet, eventually to just bark and roots, to strip himself of body fat. Once reduced to a walking bag of bones and sinews, the monk drank urushiol tea made from the Japanese lacquer tree. Much vomiting ensued, which drained the body of fluids.

Now quite ready to die, the monk was locked in a tiny stone tomb with a bell that he'd ring once a day. When the rings ceased, the tomb was sealed for a few years. Upon opening, the monk was either a mummy — bugs are evidently not interested in eating an urushiol-riddled body — or, more often, a pile of toxic goo. Travel to the Yamagata Prefecture in northern Japan to see the monks in their black, shiny, gross glory.

Urushiol Around the Globe

The wax tree, *Toxicodendron succedaneum,* is a shrubby thing over 25 feet tall that produces tons of berries. Native to the Indian sub-continent and Southeast Asia, it spread to Australia and New Zealand who classify it as a noxious weed. Its long arcing stems of flowers release urushiol-laden fumes that strafe your eyes and nose. Almost makes up for it in the fall with spectacular red foliage, so some plant it as an ornamental. But woe to those who rake the autumn leaves.

An icky yellow urushiol-rich sap oozes out of cuts made on the *Toxicodendron succedaneum* trunk. The sap is filtered and heat-treated to lessen its virulence and odor. What a fun job. The resulting wax, sometimes called Japan wax, is used to make candles and look-don't-touch hair pomades, and refined to make lacquer for artworks known as son mài in Vietnam. A super fatty-acid methyl ester in the wax makes the plant an excellent candidate for biodiesel. Except for the toxic fumes part.

One of South America's many poisonous plants, *Toxicodendron striatum*, sometimes called manzanillo, favors the lower elevations of mountains. Fortunately, its thick leaves don't leak urushiol easily. The shrubby tree produces copious amounts of small, greenish-golden apple-like fruit that get it confused with an even nastier tree, manchineel (*Hippomane mancinella*), whose poison apples can outright kill you and whose sap burns your skin off.

Rounding out the urushiol family tree are a few less common species. The Chinese varnish tree *Toxicodendron potaninii*, also called Potanin's lacquer tree, grows in far eastern China, Korea, and Japan, plus Taiwan. Small-flowered poison sumac, *Toxicodendron parviflorum*, exists in the Himalayas. Ultra rare is *Toxicodendron borneense*, a 50-foot tree in the tropical forests of Borneo. The only member of its division, *Simplicifolia*, it has large simple (not trifoliate) leaves.

Cashews, Mangos, and Toxic Treats

The genus *Toxicodendron* is part of the larger cashew family, *Anacardiaceae*. These plants are chock full of canals to transport phenolic resins like urushiol, in the case of PI and its cousins, or anacardic acid, which is as nasty as it sounds. The family offers luscious food such as mangos and cashews wrapped in toxic packaging. People who are hyper-sensitive to PI may react to mango peels, raw cashews, pistachio shells, and other *Anacardiaceae* members.

Everybody loves the cashew tree, *Anacardium occidentale*, spreading snacks and itchiness through the world for over a century. The Brazil native reaches heights of over 50 feet and is now one of the most ubiquitous trees in the tropics. It produces loads of cashew apples that look like miniature reddish-yellow butternut squashes. Lots of anacardic acid-laden leaves to wade through to pick them, but they don't break easy like PI. The astringent apples are edible if you add enough sugar or ferment them — there are so many something has to be done with them.

The yummy nut we call a cashew is a boxing glove shaped drupe growing off the end. A double shell loaded with anacardic acid surrounds the cashew. The

> For information on PI in the news and updates on products, please visit the book website:
> WWW.ITCHY.BIZ

shells are processed (and what a delight that is) to create cardanol, a phenolic lipid ultra-handy for a myriad of industrial uses. So what if it's kind of itchy to work with? Cardanol can be polymerized to near-diamond hardness. Seemed to be perfect for brake linings. An epidemic of painful respiratory rashes among brake mechanics ended that experiment. The resinous wood is termite proof, making it popular with insurers, less so with construction workers.

Mango, *Mangifera indica*, may be native to Southeast Asia, but it's now one of the most widely planted tropical trees, bringing happiness and rashes worldwide. Called the fruit of heaven and a towering 75 feet tall, the flowers release fumes that make eyes burn and noses itch. The tough mammoth leaves exude a turpentine aroma when crushed, along with a sap containing an urushiol-like allergen. It's also in the peel, especially inside the rind. After waiting months for mangos to ripen, who cares! Just wash the fruit first, give the rind a wide margin, clean the knife after peeling, and enjoy.

Brazilian pepper tree, *Schinus terebinthifolius*, also called Christmasberry, is a gorgeous and adaptable monster. Grows everywhere from desert to cropland to rainforest, as long as it's tropically warm. The low spreading shrubby tree with long coarse oval leaves can become a massive 30 to 40 foot wide block of nastiness that reeks of turpentine. Fumes from the flowers and berries feel like someone splashed acid in your face. The leaves and stems exude caustic goo as well. Cut the plant and it regrows even bushier. Huge amounts of pretty pinkish red berries spread it like crazy. Impossible to eradicate, it's now invasive in Florida. Misery, thy name is *Schinus terebinthifolius*.

Where there are dry scrub forests in the Bahamas, Caribbean or Florida Keys, there is poisonwood, *Metopium toxiferum*, containing an urushiol-like compound. The rubbery tree grows 40 feet tall with broad, tough leaves.

The genus pistacia of the *Anacardiaceae* family boasts the pistachio nut, a Middle Eastern tree cultivated worldwide. The shells or unroasted nuts might give a rash to those who are super sensitive to urushiol.

Poison Ivy and Europeans

In 1624, the British explorer John Smith learned the hard way what Native Americans had long known, but were in no mood to tell invaders: Stay away from the three-leafed plant. Smith wrote in *The Generall Historie of Virginia, New-England, and the Summer Isles*:

> "The poysoned weed is much in shape like our English Iuy, but being but touched, causeth rednesse, itching, and lastly blisters, the which howsoeuer after a while passe away of themselues without further harme, yet because for the time they are somewhat painfull, it hath got it selfe an ill name, although questionlesse of no ill nature."

The publicized warning did not dissuade plant collectors who were enthralled by the red autumn color of *Toxicodendron radicans*. The plant was taken to the Friesland area of northern Netherlands and used for erosion control on the dikes. Also kept intruders off. (Just imagine for a moment what PI would do to a Dutch person's skin. No wonder they think America is awful.) PI grows in London's Kew Gardens, the largest collection of living plants in the world.

France adored our little poison beauty, of course. Ended up in Empress Joséphine Bonaparte's gardens. Famed botanical painter Pierre-Joseph Redouté immortalized it for a French magazine cover. In the late 1700s, poison ivy got the attention of André-Ignace-Joseph Dufresnoy, a physician and professor of medicine. Convinced that something that bad just had to be good, he spent decades torturing colleagues with his "remedies."

Poison Ivy in Other Languages

Chinese: 毒藤
French: Le sumac vénéneux
German: Giftefeu
Hindi: बचिच्छु का पौधा
Italian: Edera velenosa
Japanese: ツタウルシ
Latin: Venenum hederam
Russian: ядовитый плющ
Spanish: Hiedra venenosa
Swedish: Giftig murgröna
Tajik: Айви захри

Native Americans, PI Masters — Not

It would be wonderful to regale you about Native Americans' mastery of PI. They can be PI ninjas, for sure, but claims go way beyond that. According to historic anthropology and ethnobotany books, native tribes in the western U.S. dyed basket reeds and tattooed skin with urushiol, roasted meats on poison oak stems, and wrapped food in the leaves.

A few problems with that. Are the references to *all* tribal members? Just like other races, a portion of the population is simply not allergic to urushiol. Oral history is fallible and it's easy to confuse folk names for plants. Unlike its Japanese cousin, poison oak is very hard to tap for urushiol. A lot of dangerous work adds up to a piddling amount of sap, plus it doesn't dye reeds very well. There are no cults of danger around it and Native Americans now residing in the West want nothing to do with it.

But mainly, never underestimate Native Americans' sense of humor. Toying with white people's gullibility has long been their fun. I mean really, not even the Japanese tattoo with urushiol. Adverse skin conditions are another matter. Indigenous people of the West viewed urushiol as the nuclear option for warts, ringworm, and poisonous snake bites.

Poison Oak as Art

Imagine an art show surrounded by red "Do Not Enter" tape. Such is the Poison Oak Show, held annually for over three decades in the resurrected Gold Rush mining town of Columbia, California. Let's just say alcohol is involved.

Shunted to the side patio of a saloon are the absolutely insane arrangements competitions:
- Best arrangement of poison oak.
- Best arrangement of poison oak and another plant.
- Best arrangement of poison oak and inanimate object.

The just-bragging part is also outside:
- Most potent looking green leaves.
- Most potent looking red leaves.
- Biggest branch or trunk.
- Biggest single leaf.

It gets arty:
- Best poison oak accessory or jewelry.
- Best photo of poison oak.
- Best photo of poison oak rash. (But you can enter an ongoing rash if you're willing to stand around and be ogled.)

And the most insane part of all:
- Most original poison oak dish.

No one's expected to eat it, but entrants must be serious about it. A real recipe and genuine cuisine are required. Extra points for berry usage.

As the event slogan asks: Aren't you just itchin' to participate?

Pop Culture Poison Ivy

The whining of Captain John Smith notwithstanding, poison ivy burst into pop-culture consciousness with "Poison Ivy," sung by The Coasters. It was penned by Jerry Leiber and Mike Stoller, a couple of Jewish guys who wrote much of the coolest black music of the '50s.

Very upbeat song for being about an STD (sexually transmitted disease).

Wait, you didn't know that? Do ponder the lyrics again:

> Poison ivy, poison ivy
> Late at night while you're sleepin'
> poison ivy comes a'creepin' round
>
> She's pretty as a daisy
> but look out man she's crazy
> She'll really do you in
> Now if you let her under your skin
>
> You're gonna need an ocean of calamine lotion
> You'll be scratchin' like a hound
> The minute you start to mess around

As Leiber told a magazine journalist: "Pure and simple, 'Poison Ivy' is a metaphor for a sexually transmitted disease — the clap — hardly a topic for a song that hit the Top Ten in the spring of 1959."

This dirty little ditty was covered by over a dozen groups, from the Rolling Stones to the boy band Hanson. Linda McCartney offered a bluesy take. Dave Clark Five's caffeinated version sounded like they were terrified. Billy Thorpe & The Aztecs in the '60s infused it with Beatle-like harmonies.

Oh sure, there are other poison ivy songs, not actually about the plant, of course. "Poison Ivy" by the Jonas Brothers is a banal love song. "Poison Oak" by Conor Oberst is a poetic ode to youthful idiocy. No need to understand Portuguese to know what Rita Lee's singing about in "Erva Venenosa." Search for her totally camp music video on YouTube, you won't be disappointed. Faster Pussycat's hard rock "Poison Ivy – Wake Me When It's Over" wins the prize for best song title and lyrics:

> Get off my back, you monkey
> Ya got my nerves jumping like a junkie today
> Poison ivy, ya come creepin up right behind me
> You make me itch, baby you're so unkind
> Poison ivy, you're like poison ivy
> You make me itch and I'm out of calamine

The Cramps took it one step further. They didn't do a poison ivy song. Poison Ivy played the songs. Kristy Marlana Wallace, better known as guitarist Poison Ivy Rorschach, co-founded the American punk band.

In movies, poison ivy tends toward teens. In the '90s, *Lolita* met *Fatal Attraction* in the sleazy teen thriller *Poison Ivy*. Drew Barrymore was the depraved and murderous interloper who wrecked havoc on a middle-class family. The title character continued to spread erotic misery in three trashy sequels, albeit without Barrymore. In the '80s made-for-TV comedy *Poison Ivy*, Michael J. Fox was a summer camp counselor with a crush on the nurse who treated plenty of rashes.

Poison Ivy, Batman's Nemesis

Batman had many adversaries, but none gave him such tantalizing opposition as supervillain Poison Ivy. A part of DC Comics since the mid-'60s, she was first modeled after Bettie Page, with the same bangs and Southern drawl, but red-haired. Poison Ivy quickly bloomed into a va-va-va-voom deadly beauty wearing little except strategically placed vines. In the late '90s, Uma Thurman in *Batman & Robin* took that to stratospheric levels.

Before her tragedy — all super heroes and villains have tragic histories — Poison Ivy was a brilliant botanist — comic strips love alliteration — from the Pacific Northwest. So why isn't she called Poison Oak? Nobody listens to me. A true nature lover, she was a master of plant poisons, toxins, and hypnotics. And she was, of course, very intelligent and ultra sexy because, well, comic strips.

But men turned on her, poisoning the lass with her own potions. She survived reborn as a pissed-off Poison Ivy, boasting superpowers and a heaping load of hostility toward men. Able to control all plants, Poison Ivy could make them grow huge in an instant and become animated, doing whatever she asked, like encase a man in a permanent living green jail. She was immune to any natural toxins, even fungi and bacteria, and enlisted them do her bidding as well.

Alluring and dangerous, her body exuded flowery pheromones that turned people into minions. Over time, her superpowers grew along with her curves. Her lips could kill and the vines in her clothing acquired black-belt level martial art skills. She expanded to control a global force called The Green, marshaling millions of plants in her misdeeds. In the late '80s, a new origin story for DC Comics by Neil Gaiman recast her as an acolyte of the Swamp Thing, more of a human-plant hybrid like the original Black Orchid, but imbued with the elemental mystical powers of Britain's mythical May Queen.

Poison Ivy swung between being perceived as good or evil, much like the plant. Poor thing, she just wanted to be a defender of the world's flora and fauna. But she was toxic to humans, many of whom hated her just for being who she was. Of course, she did hang out with a bad crowd of supervillains and help them do horrible things. That nasty habit of killing men who crossed her, or even lovers she tired of, didn't win her any fans. Nor did threatening to blight the world's humans because Batman wouldn't submit to her charms.

As a popular supervillain, Poison Ivy appears in dozens of Batman DC comic books, especially Suicide Squad and the Black Orchid series. A real team player, she helped other supervillains while taunting them with her superior powers. She enjoyed turning Robin into a quivering mass of protoplasm and was obsessed with Batman, who eventually tamed her into a super-frenemy. Her best friend was Harley Quinn, Joker's girlfriend, and she loved to torment him, too. Ivy's interest in Harley Quinn may have been more than friendly.

But mainly Poison Ivy vexed men. In one comic book storyline, while her first kiss was poison, the second was the antidote. She kissed Bruce Wayne, causing the dying Dark Knight to suit up and seek revenge. Weak and near death, he allowed her the kiss she craved, which brought Batman/Bruce back to life. In *Batman & Robin*, she lured Robin to her garden hideout with plans to dispatch her rival with a death kiss, but Batman made him coat his lips with rubber first. Yeah, Freudian. Also, urushiol penetrates rubber. Never mind.

Section 9 / Chapter 2

Debunking the Bull Manure

Chapter Index
- Stupid and Even Deadly Home Remedies
- Myth Busting

Few things inspire as many myths as poison oak and ivy (abbreviated in Itchy Business as PI). So much harm done by people trying to help. Even weirder, many of the hacks and home remedies are more expensive than genuine PI products off the shelf.

Stupid and Even Deadly Home Remedies

It's just amazing what people will do when they're desperate with itchiness and don't understand how the PI rash works. Some home remedies exhibit a strong masochistic streak. It's troubling, really. In every case, there is a better way. Much success attributed to home remedies really belongs to the power of placebo and the passage of time.

Home remedies come in these flavors:

Counter Irritant:
These trade one intense sensation for another. Your body and mind focuses on the new sensation, rather than the PI itch, aka the "bright shiny object" approach. Why not use counter-irritants that actually help the rash?
- Gunpowder: You keep this around?
- Iodine tincture: Go ahead, torture raw nerves.
- Hemorrhoid ointment: "Shrinks the rash." Nope, just irritates it.
- Mustard seed paste: Feel the heat, not the itch. Is that an improvement?

> The abbreviation "PI" refers to both poison oak and poison ivy.

For better counterirritants see the Cs of Rash Relief.

Numbing Agent:
Deadens nerve tips, while destroying the skin. Always prolongs the rash.
- House paint or shellac: Heavy sigh.
- Nail polish: Most contain cancerous toluene — the worst!
- Gasoline or solvents: Petrochemicals direct into open sores, are you crazy?

For better numbing agents see the Cs of Rash Relief.

Excess Alkaline:
Confuses the itch, damages the skin, prolongs the rash.
- Ammonia: "Destroys the rash." And the skin. Comparable to cleaning your bathtub with a blowtorch. A 10% solution is acceptable.
- Chlorine bleach: Ditto. A 10% solution is fine. But enough salt and baking soda has the same result while being healing.
- Wood ashes: It does set up an alkaline skin environment. And an infection.
- Lye soap: Harsh and stinky, what a combo.
- Quick lime: Just don't.

For better alkalines see Practice Safe Scratch.

Excess Acid:
Confuses the itch, hurts like hell, prolongs the rash
- Lemon juice: Ow!
- Pickle juice: Mildly acidic. Just use apple cider vinegar, unless you like being sticky.
- For better acids see Practice Safe Scratch.

General Awfulness:
- Duct tape: "Suffocates the rash." Duct tape is dirty. Anaerobic (oxygenless) infections are horrid.
- White shoe polish: Contains helpful clay and zinc oxide that is totally counteracted by the toxic petrochemicals.
- Drawing Salves: Since urushiol bonds with cellular proteins deep within the skin and oxidizes, there's nothing to draw out. Besides, do you really want to put sulfonated shale oil on you? That stuff is nasty.

For better remedies see the Cs of Rash Relief.

Somewhat Safe, Somewhat Effective:
- Urine: This one actually heals the skin a bit with urea and soothes the rash with a neutral pH. Consider using skin products with urea made from nitrogen gas, unless you think it's fun being lonely.
- Spermicide cream: Many contain benzalkonium chloride. But why not use anti-itch products with that compound? They cost less and are more effective.
- Diaper rash ointment: Contains zinc oxide, which is helpful, but most have waterproof base lotions, which are not.

For better remedies see the Cs of Rash Relief.

Myth Busting
- Plant Myths
- Identification Myths
- Exposure Myths
- Immunity Myths
- Rash Myths
- Cleaning Myths
- Protection Myths
- Assorted Myths

The more something is feared, the greater the myths about it become. PI inspires some whoppers.

Plant Myths

PI is poisonous.

It's not poisonous. It's not even toxic or caustic. It contains an allergen, urushiol, which 75% percent of the population is allergic to in the right conditions. Read more in Urushiol, Your Foe.

Bugs rest on PI leaves because it protects them from predators.

The bunnies, deer, and a myriad of other creatures that crave PI leaves relish a little extra bug protein in their meal. Read more in The American Axis of Itching.

Only the leaves are dangerous.

The entire plant except nectar and pollen is flush with urushiol. PI roots leak urushiol like a puppy pee at a dog park. Read more in Urushiol, Your Foe.

Red leaves mean more urushiol.

Young PI leaves tends toward red as do young parts of the stem. But the amount of urushiol isn't any greater, though young leaves leak urushiol easier. Leaves also turn red in the autumn. Read more in Urushiol, Your Foe.

If a PI leaf does not have black spots it's safe to touch.

Black spots show that significant amounts of urushiol has leaked out and oxidized. But urushiol operates on a molecular level and plenty can emerge from breaks too tiny to see. Read more in Know Your Adversary.

After the leaves drop in the autumn, they're safe.

Some botanists claim just prior to leaf drop urushiol and other essential nutrients are resorbed into the plant stems. In a perfect world that might be true. But how are you supposed to tell them apart from dried leaves that fell off in the summer? And a sudden frost can rip leaves from stems without time for urushiol re-absorption. Read more in Know Your Adversary.

Poison ivy always grows with jewelweed. Use the plant to remove PI from your skin and treat the rash.

If the location is wet, shady and protected, eastern poison ivy occasionally grows with jewelweed. But most of the time jewelweed is nowhere near. It goes dormant in the summer if the weather's hot and dry, and doesn't grow in the southwest at all. It won't remove urushiol off your skin any better than water and several other herbs are far superior for treating the rash. Read more in Stage 2 – Calming the Rash.

Identification Myths

Leaves of three, let them be.

Yeah, yeah, it's the leaves you don't see that get you. But PI, especially western poison oak, will very occassionally have 5 or 7 leaves. Lots of plants have leaves in triad groups. Do the leaves have scalloped, thorny or finely serrated edges (margins)? Is the middle leaf less symmetrical than the other two and lack a stem (brachis)? Are the leaf groups in opposite pairs on the stem? Do the vines have tendrils or thorns? Then it's not PI. Read more in Know Your Adversary.

Berries white, poisonous sight.

Lots of plants make white berries. Rarely white, the colors of PI berries (drupes) include beige, pale yellow, light green, and grey. The flower stems emerge from where the leaf meets the stem and dangle downward, so berries are rarely seen until leaf drop. Read more in The American Axis of Itching.

Hairy vine, no friend of mine.

Of the four PI species, eastern poison ivy produces a tremendous amount of vines, western poison oak often does, and western poison ivy and eastern poison oak never do. Only vines that are ascending a tree or object create the hairy aerial roots, not ground vines. But those roots appear only on older climbing vines. Read more in The American Axis of Itching.

Red leaflets in spring, a poisonous thing.

New growth in PI is often quite red, but not always. More green leaf surface enables greater photosynthesis, so PI in dim light often has less red. Read more in Know Your Adversary.

Side leaves like mittens, itch like the dickens.

That's often true for eastern poison ivy, but even it has subspecies with deeply lobed leaves that look like some oaks, or long thin leaves that appear like willows. Western poison oak leaves have astounding variety. But the middle leaf will always be more symmetrical, have a longer stem (brachis), and alternate on the main stem. Read more in Know Your Adversary.

Exposure Myths

I got the rash by standing near PI.

Giant ragweed in pollen season, for instance, can cause a rash wothout touching — and it itches like the dickens. The only way to get a PI rash by proxy is to inhale the smoke of its burning, like in a wildfire or bonfire. The entire respiratory system reacts; sometimes the throat and nose swell shut. People have died. It's horrible. Read more in Urushiol, Your Foe.

I was nowhere close to PI and still got a rash.

Welcome to secondary exposure. Urushiol is ferried to your skin by dogs and objects that have a splotch of urushiol atop them. The stuff never evaporates and takes centuries (no joke) to become inactive. Read more in Urushiol, Your Foe.

My tent was in storage for over a decade and I still got PI from it.

That is completely possible. A thorough detergent cleaning of all camping gear when you get home is a very good practice. Read more in Prevent Secondary Exposure.

Immunity Myths

You can build up resistance to urushiol by ingesting it.

Urushiol operates on a molecular level. The amount on the head of a pin can give rashes to thousands of people. Still think eating it will do anything except do permanent damage to your body? Read more in Urushiol, Your Foe.

Once allergic, always allergic to PI.
Some people are not allergic to PI at all.
You can develop immunity from repeat exposure.

Immunity comes and immunity goes. The immune system you have at age 8 is far different from what you have in your 30s, which isn't like the one you have as a senior over 65. As your immune system changes, so does your immunity. Flaunt your immunity at your own risk. Read more in Urushiol, Your Foe.

I'm allergic to poison oak but not poison ivy.

Poison oak and poison ivy differ very slightly chemically, but not enough to matter. More likely you were exposed to poison oak when you had recently bathed or it was hot and humid — both enhance absorption of urushiol. Read more in Urushiol, Your Foe.

Rash Myths

I touched PI and got an instant rash.

PI is an insidious delayed-reaction rash because it's an allergic rash, not a contact rash. It takes time for the urushiol to seep into the dermis layer of the skin and reach the immune system. But if on thin skin like the face or inner arm, it can be absorbed in as soon as 15 minutes. If a rash happens that quickly, go to the emergency room ASAP — it indicates real medical trouble. Read more in When the Rash Goes Bad.

PI rash is contagious.

As long as you've thoroughly cleaned after urushiol exposure, rub your naked body against anyone else's naked body and they won't get a rash. But they will get excited. Read more in Rash 101.

The rash spread all over me again when the blisters popped.

By the time you have blisters from PI, the urushiol is bonded, oxidized and gone gone gone. Blister fluid is just lymph juices and blood serum, icky but nontoxic. A light touch of PI will take longer to manifest as a rash, making it seem like it spread. Or you re-exposed yourself from urushiol lurking on your pet, on objects used outdoors, or brought inside the home or office. Read more in Rash 101.

Poison ivy can go systemic.

It's not as if urushiol can be carried throughout the body. It bonds in the dermis layer of skin, so it can't. But it reacts with the lymph system, integral to the body's immune defense, and enough urushiol can throw it into extreme uproar. A bad enough rash, or a rash covering more than 25% of the body, can awaken old rash sites of all kinds. Just awful. Read more in When the Rash Goes Bad.

You can get a PI rash from mangos.

An urushiol-like compound lurks in the rinds of mangos that those sensitive to urushiol can be allergic to. Occasionally that compound is on the outside. So wash the mango first, be careful with the knife you use, and give the rind a wide berth. The same compound is in the shells of cashews and to a lesser degree pistachios, so the raw nuts can have some on them. Wash them first, too, and roast thoroughly. Read more in Strange Facts and Terrible Tales.

For information on PI in the news and updates on products, please visit the book website:

WWW.ITCHY.BIZ

Cleaning Myths

I took a shower and spread urushiol all over me.

A hot shower immediately after exposure might do that. But urushiol bonds to proteins in the dermis layer of the skin within 15 minutes to a few hours, and once bonded it's not going anywhere with just soap and water. Read more in Cleaning Off Urushiol.

Just put some dirt on it. That will absorb the urushiol.

Much more likely to press it further into your skin. Urushiol is a resin, so it's not very absorptive. Think of it as a microscopic blob. The best technique if caught immediately is to roll it off your skin with a fluid. Read more in Cleaning Off Urushiol.

I used poison ivy soap and washed it right off.

If it's a very light touch of PI that's still atop the skin, yes. If the urushiol was pressed into the skin, no. Soap lacks enough surfactants, which lift the offending substance to the surface of the water. Nor does soap penetrate the epidermis deeply. The right detergents are packed with surfactants and reach easily into the epidermis. Read more in Cleaning Off Urushiol.

Jewelweed will remove urushiol from the skin.

The only way jewelweed could do that if you squeezed the plant's juice on it. In that case, it's the fluid that washed it off rather than any special qualities of the plant. Only strong detergents and special PI solvents and scrubs remove urushiol from the skin. But herbs can be excellent in treating the rash. Read more in Cleaning Off Urushiol.

You can just rinse urushiol off stuff.

That's mostly true, but even new items have cracks and divots where urushiol can hide. A detergent or PI solvent bath is best. Absorptive things like clothing need multiple cleanings with a strong detergent, preferably in a washing machine. Read more in Cleaning Off Urushiol.

Protection Myths

Just coat yourself in spray deodorant OR liquid bandage OR any other home hacks.

Urushiol operates on a molecular level. Skin coatings must be highly specific to block it. Currently in vogue as a PI barrier lotion is a super-tight polymer with a high positive charge. Read more in Prevent Skin Contact.

Clothing will block urushiol.

Sometimes. For a short while. But on a hot day, a tight t-shirt or dew-rag can spread urushiol around via your sweat. Wicking fabric is best for close-to-the-body clothing. Read more in Prevent Skin Contact.

Wear rubber (or latex) gloves to pull up the plant.

Urushiol soaks right through rubber or latex. Vinyl and nitrile gloves are your friends. Read more in Prevent Skin Contact.

Assorted Myths

Only humans get PI rashes.

Yep. We lost our fur and gained an allergy to PI. A few small hairless primates are sensitive to the plant. Read more in Poison Oak and Poison Ivy: Weirder Than You Know.

There is nothing good about PI.

PI is a smart and ancient plant, changing and adapting as needed, filling niches and needs. Its extensive root and rhizome stalls erosion along creeks and gullies. Larger climbing vines provide superb nesting for birds and raccoons. Birds and other wildlife enjoy the berries that linger on the stem, lasting well into winter. The leaves provide high protein browse for deer and rabbits. What's not to like? Except the rash thing. Read more in Poison Oak and Poison Ivy: Weirder Than You Know.

Resources

Section Index
1. Bibliography
2. Illustration and Photo Credits
3. About the Author

Bibliography

SECTION 1
The Big Itchy Picture

Poison oak and ivy (PI) are endlessly fascinating plants. Botanists like William Epstein and William T. Gillis are the elder statesmen of PI. Modern immunology has grasped this complex allergic reaction and the future potential for taming it is good. But when it comes to understanding and treating the rash, pediatric nursing, emergency and wilderness medicine are at the forefront. You'll see these core references repeated often.

Section 1 / Chapter 1
Poison Oak and Poison Ivy: Weirder Than You Know

General sources of information

Leaves of Three, Let Them Be: If Only It Were That Easy
by Patricia L. Jackson Allen, MS, RN PNP, FAAN
Pediatric Nursing 2004;30(2)
http://www.medscape.com/viewarticle/475190_3

Poison Ivy: an Exaggerated Immune Response to Nothing Much
Biology Department, University of Massachusetts, March 31, 1997
http://www.bio.umass.edu/micro/immunology/poisoniv.htm

Poison-ivy and Its Kin
by William T. Gillis
Arnoldia, the journal of the Arnold Arboretum at Harvard University, 1975
http://arnoldia.arboretum.harvard.edu/pdf/articles/1975-35-2-poison-ivy-and-its-kin.pdf

Poison Oak: More Than Just Scratching The Surface
updated by W.P. Armstrong
January 16, 2011
http://waynesword.palomar.edu/ww0802.htm

Poison Oak: More Than Just Scratching The Surface
by W.P. Armstrong and W.L. Epstein, M.D.
Herbalgram (American Botanical Council) Volume 34: 36-42, 1995

Toxicodendron Dermatitis: Poison Ivy, Oak, and Sumac
by Aaron C. Gladman, MD, Department of Emergency Medicine, Harbor-UCLA Medical Center, Torrance, CA
June 2006, Volume 17, Issue 2, Pages 120–128
http://www.wemjournal.org/article/S1080-6032%2806%2970299-X/fulltext

Specialized sources of information: Four main poison oak and ivy species

Eastern poison ivy, *Toxicodendron radicans*
http://plants.usda.gov/core/profile?symbol=TORA2
http://www.fs.fed.us/database/feis/plants/shrub/toxspp/all.html

Eastern poison oak, *Toxicodendron pubescens*
http://plants.usda.gov/java/profile?symbol=TOPU2
http://www.fs.fed.us/database/feis/plants/shrub/toxpub/all.html

Rydberg's poison ivy, *Toxicodendron rydbergii*
http://plants.usda.gov/java/profile?symbol=TORY
http://www.fs.fed.us/database/feis/plants/shrub/toxspp/all.html
http://www.fs.fed.us/global/iitf/pdf/shrubs/Toxicodendron%20rydbergii.pdf

Western poison oak, *Toxicodendron diversilobum*
http://plants.usda.gov/java/profile?symbol=TODI
http://www.fs.fed.us/database/feis/plants/vine/toxdiv/all.html

Specialized sources of information: Captain John Smith and poison ivy

The Generall Historie of Virginia, New-England, and the Summer Isles
by Captain John Smith
http://www.americanjourneys.org/pdf/AJ-082.pdf

Specialized sources of information: Global warming and poison ivy

Poison Ivy, Now With Stronger Poison
by Mike Nizza
The New York Times, The Lede, June 27, 2007
http://thelede.blogs.nytimes.com/2007/06/27/poison-ivy-now-with-stronger-poison

SECTION 2
Understanding Urushiol

Deep botanical nerdiness on the allergen contained in poison oak and ivy, plus the science of cleaning this microscopic foe.

Section 2 / Chapters 1 - 2
Urushiol, Your Foe
Cleaning Off Urushiol

General sources of information

The diagnostic evaluation, treatment, and prevention of allergic contact dermatitis in the new millennium
by Donald V. Belsito, MD
Journal of Allergy and Clinical Immunology, Volume 105, Issue 3, March 2000, Pages 409–420
http://www.jacionline.org/article/S0091-6749%2800%2994189-7/abstract

Leaves of Three, Let Them Be: If Only It Were That Easy
by Patricia L. Jackson Allen, MS, RN PNP, FAAN
Pediatric Nursing 2004;30(2)
http://www.medscape.com/viewarticle/475190_3

Poison Oak: More Than Just Scratching The Surface
updated by W.P. Armstrong
January 16, 2011
http://waynesword.palomar.edu/ww0802.htm

Poison Oak: More Than Just Scratching The Surface
by W.P. Armstrong and W.L. Epstein, M.D.
Herbalgram (American Botanical Council) Volume 34: 36-42, 1995

Poison-ivy and Its Kin
by William T. Gillis
Arnoldia, the journal of the Arnold Arboretum at Harvard University, 1975
http://arnoldia.arboretum.harvard.edu/pdf/articles/1975-35-2-poison-ivy-and-its-kin.pdf

Toxicodendron Dermatitis: Poison Ivy, Oak, and Sumac
by Aaron C. Gladman, MD, Department of Emergency Medicine, Harbor-UCLA Medical Center, Torrance, CA
June 2006, Volume 17, Issue 2, Pages 120–128
http://www.wemjournal.org/article/S1080-6032%2806%2970299-X/fulltext

Specialized sources of information: Cleaning urushiol

Cost-effective post-exposure prevention of poison ivy dermatitis
by Stibich AS1, Yagan M, Sharma V, Herndon B, Montgomery C.
International Journal of Dermatolgy 2000 Jul;39(7):515-8
http://www.ncbi.nlm.nih.gov/pubmed/10940115

Detergent
https://en.wikipedia.org/wiki/Detergent

Effective Topical Treatment and Post Exposure Prophylaxis of Poison Ivy: Objective Confirmation
by H. Stankewicz , G. Cancel , M. Eberhardt , S. Melanson St. Lukes Hospital, Bethlehem, PA
September 2007Volume 50, Issue 3, Supplement, Pages S26–S27 81

http://www.zanfel.com/admin/documents/ZAN117-St.%20Lukes%202007%20Study_20150501.pdf

Surfactant
https://en.wikipedia.org/wiki/Surfactant

Toxicodendron Dermatitis: Poison Ivy, Oak, and Sumac
by Aaron C. Gladman, MD, Department of Emergency Medicine, Harbor-UCLA Medical Center, Torrance, CA
June 2006, Volume 17, Issue 2, Pages 120–128
http://www.wemjournal.org/article/S1080-6032%2806%2970299-X/fulltext

Specialized sources of information: Desensitization to urushiol

Complexing urushiols
by R.A. Sanchez, S.S. Hendler - US Patent 5,409,908, 1995
http://www.google.com/patents/US5767109

Immunologic Studies of Poisonous Anacardiaceae: Oral Desensitization to Poison Ivy and Oak Urushiols in Guinea Pigs
by Edna S. Watson, James C. Murphy and Mahmoud A. El Sohly, Research Institute of Pharmaceutical Sciences, School of Pharmacy, University of Mississippi, University, Mississippi, U.S.A. Accepted July 28, 1982
http://www.nature.com/jid/journal/v80/n3/abs/5615240a.html

Induction of Tolerance to Poison Ivy Urushiol in the Geunia Pig by Epicutaneous Application of the Structural Analog 5-Methyl-3-n-Pentadecylcatechol
by J-L Stampf, et al
Journal of Investigative Dermatology, 1986, 86: pg. 535-538
http://www.ncbi.nlm.nih.gov/pubmed/2943824

An Oral Antigen Preparation in the Prevention of Poison Ivy Dermatitis
by Elmer R. Gross, M.D.
Industrial Medicine and Surgery, 27:3, 142-144, March, 1958
http://www.ncbi.nlm.nih.gov/pubmed/13513172

Suppression of Urushiol-Induced Delayed-Type Hypersensitivity Responses in Mice with Serum IgG Immunoglobulin from Human Hyposensitized Donors
by J-L. Stampf, N. Castagnoli, W. L. Epstein, et al
Journal of Investigative Dermatology, 1990, 95: 363-365
http://www.ncbi.nlm.nih.gov/pubmed/2384694

SECTION 3
Rash Mastery

Conveying deep medical knowledge about skin and the body's immune and neurological systems in order to master the rash and realize when it's out of control.

Section 3 / Chapters 1 - 3
Rash 101
It's All About That Itch
When the Rash Goes Bad

General sources of information

The diagnostic evaluation, treatment, and prevention of allergic contact dermatitis in the new millennium
by Donald V. Belsito, MD
Journal of Allergy and Clinical Immunology, Volume 105, Issue 3, March 2000, Pages 409–420
http://www.jacionline.org/article/S0091-6749%2800%2994189-7/abstract

Leaves of Three, Let Them Be: If Only It Were That Easy
by Patricia L. Jackson Allen, MS, RN PNP, FAAN
Pediatric Nursing 2004;30(2)
http://www.medscape.com/viewarticle/475190_3

Poison Ivy: an Exaggerated Immune Response to Nothing Much
Biology Department, University of Massachusetts, March 31, 1997
http://www.bio.umass.edu/micro/immunology/poisoniv.htm

Toxicodendron Dermatitis: Poison Ivy, Oak, and Sumac
by Aaron C. Gladman, MD, Department of Emergency Medicine, Harbor-UCLA Medical Center, Torrance, CA
June 2006, Volume 17, Issue 2, Pages 120–128
http://www.wemjournal.org/article/S1080-6032%2806%2970299-X/fulltext

Specialized sources of information: Itch

Itching
MedLinePlus, U.S. National Library of Medicine
https://www.nlm.nih.gov/medlineplus/ency/article/003217.htm

How the Itch Informs the Scratch
Scientific American podcast
http://www.scientificamerican.com/podcast/episode/how-the-itch-informs-the-scratch-12-01-28/

Itching for Relief
American Academy of Dermatology
https://www.aad.org/login?ReturnUrl=/dw/monthly/2015/february/itching-for-relief

Why Does Scratching An Itch Make It Worse?
by Justine Alford
IFL Science, November 3, 2014
http://www.iflscience.com/health-and-medicine/why-does-scratching-itch-make-it-worse

Specialized sources of information: Skin

Human skin
Encyclopædia Britannica
http://www.britannica.com/science/human-skin

Skin layers
University of Maryland Medical Center
http://umm.edu/health/medical/ency/images/skin-layers

SECTION 4
Your Rash Toolkit

Much of this section relies on my personal experience with the poison ivy rash, but the scratch chapter is based on great itch science. The plant and mineral glossary is botanical nerdism at its best with a touch of chemistry tossed in.

Section 4 / Chapters 1 - 4
Practice Safe Scratch

The Stages: Your Key To Rash Relief

The Cs of Itch Relief

Plants and Minerals

General sources of information

A Critical Review of Herbal Remedies for Poison Ivy Dermatitis
by David S. Senchina
American Botanical Council HerbalGram. 2005; Issue: 66 Page: 35-48
http://cms.herbalgram.org/herbalgram/issue66/article2830.html

The diagnostic evaluation, treatment, and prevention of allergic contact dermatitis in the new millennium
by Donald V. Belsito, MD
Journal of Allergy and Clinical Immunology, Volume 105, Issue 3, March 2000, Pages 409–420
http://www.jacionline.org/article/S0091-6749%2800%2994189-7/abstract

Leaves of Three, Let Them Be: If Only It Were That Easy
by Patricia L. Jackson Allen, MS, RN PNP, FAAN
Pediatric Nursing 2004;30(2)
http://www.medscape.com/viewarticle/475190_3

Toxicodendron Dermatitis: Poison Ivy, Oak, and Sumac
by Aaron C. Gladman, MD, Department of Emer-

gency Medicine, Harbor-UCLA Medical Center, Torrance, CA
June 2006, Volume 17, Issue 2, Pages 120–128
http://www.wemjournal.org/article/S1080-6032%2806%2970299-X/fulltext

Specialized sources of information: Itch

Itching
MedLinePlus, U.S. National Library of Medicine
https://www.nlm.nih.gov/medlineplus/ency/article/003217.htm

How the Itch Informs the Scratch
Scientific American podcast
http://www.scientificamerican.com/podcast/episode/how-the-itch-informs-the-scratch-12-01-28/

Itching for Relief
American Academy of Dermatology
https://www.aad.org/login?ReturnUrl=/dw/monthly/2015/february/itching-for-relief

Why Does Scratching An Itch Make It Worse?
by Justine Alford
IFL Science, November 3, 2014
http://www.iflscience.com/health-and-medicine/why-does-scratching-itch-make-it-worse

Specialized sources of information: Pharmaceuticals and prescriptions

Benzocaine Information
http://www.fda.gov/drugs/drugsafety/postmarketdrugsafetyinformationforpatientsandproviders/ucm273111.htm

Benzyl alcohol
https://en.wikipedia.org/wiki/Benzyl_alcohol

Hailed and Feared, Cortisone Now Safer and More Varied
by Jane Brody, January 20, 1981
http://www.nytimes.com/1981/01/20/science/hailed-and-feared-cortisone-now-safer-and-more-varied.html

Labeling of Diphenhydramine-Containing Drug Products for Over- the-Counter Human Use
Food and Drug Administration
21 CFR Parts 336, 338, and 341 [Docket No. 97N-0128]
http://www.fda.gov/ohrms/dockets/98fr/120602a.htm

Methylprednisolone
http://www.drugs.com/methylprednisolone.html

Methylprednisolone Oral
https://www.nlm.nih.gov/medlineplus/druginfo/meds/a682795.html

Pramoxine
https://www.nlm.nih.gov/medlineplus/druginfo/meds/a682429.html

Specialized sources of information: Plant-based compounds

Active principles of Grindelia robusta exert antiinflammatory properties in a macrophage model
by La VD1, Lazzarin F, Ricci D, Fraternale D, Genovese S, Epifano F, Grenier D.
Phytotherapy Research, 2010 Nov;24(11):1687-92. doi: 10.1002/ptr.3195.

Adverse and beneficial effects of plant extracts on skin and skin disorders
Adverse Drug Reaction Toxicology Review. 2001 Jun;20(2):89-103.
by Mantle D, Gok MA, Lennard TW.
http://www.ncbi.nlm.nih.gov/pubmed/11482001

Anti-inflammatory activities of colloidal oatmeal (Avena sativa) contribute to the effectiveness of oats in treatment of itch associated with dry, irritated skin
by Reynertson KA, Garay M, Nebus J, Chon S, Kaur S, Mahmood K, Kizoulis M, Southall MD.
Journal of Drugs for Dermatology, 2015 Jan;14(1):43-8.
http://www.ncbi.nlm.nih.gov/pubmed/25607907

Avena sativa (Oat), a potential neutraceutical and therapeutic agent: an overview
by Singh R1, De S, Belkheir A.
Critical Review of Food Science and Nutrition,

2013;53(2):126-44. doi: 10.1080/10408398.2010.526725.
http://www.ncbi.nlm.nih.gov/pubmed/23072529

Case Report of Gumweed in Treatment of Poison Oak Dermatitis
by Mariann Garner-Wizard
HerbClip, Date: September 29, 2006, HC# 010561-313
http://cms.herbalgram.org/herbclip/313/review44546.html

Chamomile: A herbal medicine of the past with bright future
by Janmejai K Srivastava, Eswar Shankar, and Sanjay Gupta
Mol Med Report. 2010 Nov 1; 3(6): 895–901. doi: 10.3892/mmr.2010.377
http://www.ncbi.nlm.nih.gov/pmc/articles/PMC2995283/#

The effect of jewel weed in preventing poison ivy dermatitis
by B.J. Zink, E.J. Orren, M. Rosenthal and B. Singal, Department of Emergency Medicine, Albany Medical College
Journal of Wilderness Medicine 2, 178-182 (1991)
http://www.wemjournal.org/article/S0953-9859%2891%2970066-1/pdf

Helichrysum italicum: The Sleeping Giant of Mediterranean Herbal Medicine
by Giovanni, PhD Appendino, Orazio Taglialatela-Scafati, PhD, Alberto Minassi, PhD, Federica Pollastro, PhD, Laurea Mauro Ballero, Andrea Maxia, PhD, Cinzia Sanna, PhD
HerbalGram. 2015; American Botanical Council; Issue: 105 Page: 34-45
http://cms.herbalgram.org/herbalgram/issue105/hg105-feat-helichrysum.html

Herbal Anti-Inflammatory Agents for Skin Disease
by J. Graf, MD Department of Dermatology, New York University Medical Center, New York
Skin Therapy Letter, 2000/5.4/2
http://www.skintherapyletter.com/2000/5.4/2.html

Review of Horse Chestnut (Aesculus hippocastanum) Clinical Trials
by ¡XHeather S. Oliff, Ph.D
HerbClip, American Botanical Council; Date: October 31, 2002, HC# 050822-219
http://cms.herbalgram.org/herbclip/219/review43165.html

Review of Witch Hazel (Hamamelis virginiana)
by Zeylstra, H.
British Journal of Phytotherapy, Date: February 08, 1999, HC# 101283-150
http://cms.herbalgram.org/herbclip/150/review41666.html?ts=1456536439&signature=40c-6671ba79f522b2bb79a800322d619

Side Effects of Herbal Drugs Used in Dermatologic Disorders
by Gita Faghihi, Mohammadreza Radan
Journal of Cosmetics, Dermatological Sciences and Applications
Vol.1 No.1(2011), Article ID:4110
http://file.scirp.org/Html/q%201050001_4110.htm

Successful Treatment of Poison Oak Dermatitis Treated with Grindelia spp. (Gumweed)
by Don Canavan and Eric Yarnell
The Journal of Alternative and Complementary Medicine. August 2005, 11(4): 709-710. doi:10.1089/acm.2005.11.709. Volume: 11 Issue 4: August 30, 2005
http://online.liebertpub.com/doi/abs/10.1089/acm.2005.11.709

Specialized sources of information: Plant glossaries

American Botanical Council: HerbalGram and HerbClip
http://abc.herbalgram.org/

Herb Pharm: plant library
http://www.herb-pharm.com/products/herbs-a-to-z

Herb Research Foundation: archives
http://www.herbs.org/herbnews/

Mountain Rose Herbs: plant library
https://www.mountainroseherbs.com/catalog/herbs/bulk

National Library of Medicine: Herb Garden
https://www.nlm.nih.gov/about/herbgarden/list.html

Specialized sources of information: Psychology

Attacked by Poison Ivy: A Psychological Understanding
by Ann Belford Ulanov
Nicolas-Hays (November 2001)

SECTION 5
Rash Remedies

More of my personal experience to the fore here, featuring my unique four-stage approach to healing the rash via the C's of rash relief: calm, cool, constrict.

Section 5 / Chapters 1-8
Rash Re-Cap

Stage 1 – Interrupting the Rash

Stage 2 – Calming the Rash

Stage 2 – Cooling the Itch

Stage 3 – Constricting the Blisters

Stages 2 and 3 – Analgesics for Pain Relief

Stage 4 – Repairing the Skin

Holistic: Treat the Body, Reduce the Rash

General sources of information

A Critical Review of Herbal Remedies for Poison Ivy Dermatitis
by David S. Senchina
American Botanical Council HerbalGram. 2005; Issue: 66 Page: 35-48
http://cms.herbalgram.org/herbalgram/issue66/article2830.html

The diagnostic evaluation, treatment, and prevention of allergic contact dermatitis in the new millennium
by Donald V. Belsito, MD
Journal of Allergy and Clinical Immunology, Volume 105, Issue 3, March 2000, Pages 409–420
http://www.jacionline.org/article/S0091-6749%2800%2994189-7/abstract

Leaves of Three, Let Them Be: If Only It Were That Easy
by Patricia L. Jackson Allen, MS, RN PNP, FAAN
Pediatric Nursing 2004;30(2)
http://www.medscape.com/viewarticle/475190_3

Toxicodendron Dermatitis: Poison Ivy, Oak, and Sumac
by Aaron C. Gladman, MD, Department of Emergency Medicine, Harbor-UCLA Medical Center, Torrance, CA
June 2006, Volume 17, Issue 2, Pages 120–128
http://www.wemjournal.org/article/S1080-6032%2806%2970299-X/fulltext

Specialized sources of information: Analgesics

Benzocaine Information
http://www.fda.gov/drugs/drugsafety/postmarketdrugsafetyinformationforpatientsandproviders/ucm273111.htm

Benzyl alcohol
https://en.wikipedia.org/wiki/Benzyl_alcohol

Pramoxine
https://www.nlm.nih.gov/medlineplus/druginfo/meds/a682429.html

Specialized sources of information: Plant glossaries

American Botanical Council: HerbalGram and HerbClip
http://abc.herbalgram.org/

Herb Pharm: plant library
http://www.herb-pharm.com/products/herbs-a-to-z

Herb Research Foundation: archives
http://www.herbs.org/herbnews/

Mountain Rose Herbs: plant library
https://www.mountainroseherbs.com/catalog/herbs/bulk

National Library of Medicine: Herb Garden
https://www.nlm.nih.gov/about/herbgarden/list.html

Specialized sources of information: Psychology

Attacked by Poison Ivy: A Psychological Understanding
by Ann Belford Ulanov
Nicolas-Hays (November 2001)

SECTION 6
Identifying the Plant

Most botanical information on poison oak and ivy appearance, propagation, growing habits, habitat, range, and wildlife use comes from the PLANTS Database of the Natural Resources Conservation Service division of the U.S. Department of Agriculture. The U.S. Forest Service Fire Effects Information Systems plant database has good additional field information.

Section 6 / Chapters 1- 2
The American Axis of Itching
Know Your Adversary

General sources of information

Poison-ivy and Its Kin
by William T. Gillis
Arnoldia, the journal of the Arnold Arboretum at Harvard University, 1975
http://arnoldia.arboretum.harvard.edu/pdf/articles/1975-35-2-poison-ivy-and-its-kin.pdf

Poison Oak: More Than Just Scratching The Surface
by W.P. Armstrong and W.L. Epstein, M.D.
Herbalgram (American Botanical Council) Volume 34: 36-42, 1995

Poison Oak: More Than Just Scratching The Surface
updated by W.P. Armstrong
January 16, 2011
http://waynesword.palomar.edu/ww0802.htm

Toxicodendron Dermatitis: Poison Ivy, Oak, and Sumac
by Aaron C. Gladman, MD, Department of Emergency Medicine, Harbor-UCLA Medical Center, Torrance, CA
June 2006, Volume 17, Issue 2, Pages 120–128
http://www.wemjournal.org/article/S1080-6032%2806%2970299-X/fulltext

Specialized sources of information: The four main species

Eastern poison ivy, *Toxicodendron radicans*
http://plants.usda.gov/core/profile?symbol=TORA2
http://www.fs.fed.us/database/feis/plants/shrub/toxspp/all.html

Eastern poison oak, *Toxicodendron pubescens*
http://plants.usda.gov/java/profile?symbol=TOPU2
http://www.fs.fed.us/database/feis/plants/shrub/toxpub/all.html

Rydberg's poison ivy, *Toxicodendron rydbergii*
http://plants.usda.gov/java/profile?symbol=TORY
http://www.fs.fed.us/database/feis/plants/shrub/toxspp/all.html
http://www.fs.fed.us/global/iitf/pdf/shrubs/Toxicodendron%20rydbergii.pdf

Western poison oak, *Toxicodendron diversilobum*
http://plants.usda.gov/java/profile?symbol=TODI
http://www.fs.fed.us/database/feis/plants/vine/toxdiv/all.html

Specialized sources of information: Poison oak and ivy imitators

Aromatic sumac (Rhus aromatica)
http://plants.usda.gov/core/profile?symbol=RHAR4

Blackberry family (Rubus)
http://plants.usda.gov/core/profile?symbol=RUBUS

Bladdernut (Staphylea trifolia)
http://plants.usda.gov/core/profile?symbol=STTR

Boston ivy (Parthenocissus tricuspidata)
http://plants.usda.gov/core/profile?symbol=PATR6

Box elder (Acer negundo)
http://plants.usda.gov/core/profile?symbol=ACNE2

Hop tree (Ptelea trifoliata)
http://plants.usda.gov/core/profile?symbol=PTTR

Jack in the pulpit (Arisaema triphyllum)
http://plants.usda.gov/core/profile?symbol=ARTR

Sassafras (Sassafras albidum)
http://plants.usda.gov/core/profile?symbol=SAAL5

Virginia creeper (Parthenocissus quinquefolia)
http://plants.usda.gov/core/profile?symbol=PAQU2

Specialized sources of information: Poison sumac

Toxicodendron vernix (poison sumac)
http://plants.usda.gov/core/profile?symbol=TOVE

SECTION 7
Defending Yourself

Section 7 / Chapters 1 - 2
Prevent Skin Contact
Prevent Secondary Exposure

General sources of information:

Leaves of Three, Let Them Be: If Only It Were That Easy
by Patricia L. Jackson Allen, MS, RN PNP, FAAN
Pediatric Nursing 2004;30(2)
http://www.medscape.com/viewarticle/475190_3

Poison Oak and Poison Ivy Dermatitis: Prevention and Treat in Forest Service Work
by W.L. Epstein. and V.S. Byers
U.S. Dept. of Agriculture Forest Service, publication 8167 2803 (1981)

Poison-ivy and Its Kin
by William T. Gillis
Arnoldia, the journal of the Arnold Arboretum at Harvard University, 1975
http://arnoldia.arboretum.harvard.edu/pdf/articles/1975-35-2-poison-ivy-and-its-kin.pdf

Poison Oak: More Than Just Scratching The Surface
updated by W.P. Armstrong
January 16, 2011
http://waynesword.palomar.edu/ww0802.htm

Poison Oak: More Than Just Scratching The Surface
by W.P. Armstrong and W.L. Epstein, M.D.
Herbalgram (American Botanical Council) Volume 34: 36-42, 1995

Poison Oak and Poison Ivy Dermatitis: Prevention and Treat in Forest Service Work
by W.L. Epstein. and V.S. Byers
U.S. Dept. of Agriculture Forest Service, publication 8167 2803 (1981)

Specialized sources of information: Cleaning urushiol

Detergent
https://en.wikipedia.org/wiki/Detergent

Effective Topical Treatment and Post Exposure Prophylaxis of Poison Ivy: Objective Confirmation
by H. Stankewicz, G. Cancel, M. Eberhardt, S. Melanson St. Lukes Hospital, Bethlehem, PA
September 2007Volume 50, Issue 3, Supplement, Pages S26–S27 81
http://www.zanfel.com/admin/documents/ZAN117-St.%20Lukes%202007%20Study_20150501.pdf

Surfactant
https://en.wikipedia.org/wiki/Surfactant

Toxicodendron Dermatitis: Poison Ivy, Oak, and Sumac
  by Aaron C. Gladman, MD, Department of Emergency Medicine, Harbor-UCLA Medical Center, Torrance, CA
  June 2006, Volume 17, Issue 2, Pages 120–128
  http://www.wemjournal.org/article/S1080-6032%2806%2970299-X/fulltext

Specialized sources of information: Preventing urushiol contact

Cost-effective post-exposure prevention of poison ivy dermatitis
  by Stibich AS1, Yagan M, Sharma V, Herndon B, Montgomery C.
  International Journal of Dermatolgy 2000 Jul;39(7):515-8
  http://www.ncbi.nlm.nih.gov/pubmed/10940115

Outsmarting Poison Ivy and Its Cousins
  FDA Consumer, Sept. 1996
  http://www.fda.gov/fdac/features/796_ivy.html

Poison Oak and Poison Ivy Dermatitis: Prevention and Treat in Forest Service Work
  by W.L. Epstein. and V.S. Byers
  U.S. Dept. of Agriculture Forest Service, publication 8167 2803 (1981)

SECTION 8
Eradicating the Plant

Section 8 / Chapters 1 - 2
Prepare for Battle
Bye, Bye, PI

Specialized sources of information: Four main poison oak and ivy species

Eastern poison ivy, *Toxicodendron radicans*
  http://plants.usda.gov/core/profile?symbol=TORA2
  http://www.fs.fed.us/database/feis/plants/shrub/toxspp/all.html

Eastern poison oak, *Toxicodendron pubescens*
  http://plants.usda.gov/java/profile?symbol=TOPU2
  http://www.fs.fed.us/database/feis/plants/shrub/toxpub/all.html

Rydberg's poison ivy, *Toxicodendron rydbergii*
  http://plants.usda.gov/java/profile?symbol=TORY
  http://www.fs.fed.us/database/feis/plants/shrub/toxspp/all.html
  http://www.fs.fed.us/global/iitf/pdf/shrubs/Toxicodendron%20rydbergii.pdf

Western poison oak, *Toxicodendron diversilobum*
  http://plants.usda.gov/java/profile?symbol=TODI
  http://www.fs.fed.us/database/feis/plants/vine/toxdiv/all.html

Specialized sources of information: Eradicating the plant

Acetic acid (vinegar) for weed control revisited
  http://www.weeds.iastate.edu/weednews/vinegar.htm

Herbicides
  https://www3.epa.gov/caddis/ssr_herb_int.html

Orange oil
  https://en.wikipedia.org/wiki/Orange_oil

Selective, Post-Emergent Weed controls
  http://www.growsmartgrowsafe.org/Products.aspx

Vinegar as a burn-down herbicide: Acetic acid concentrations, application volumes, and adjuvants
  http://www.ars.usda.gov/research/publications/publications.htm?seq_no_115=195808

Specialized sources of information: Preventing urushiol contact

Cost-effective post-exposure prevention of poison ivy dermatitis
  by Stibich AS1, Yagan M, Sharma V, Herndon B, Montgomery C.
  International Journal of Dermatolgy 2000 Jul;39(7):515-8
  http://www.ncbi.nlm.nih.gov/pubmed/10940115

Outsmarting Poison Ivy and Its Cousins
FDA Consumer, Sept. 1996
http://www.fda.gov/fdac/features/796_ivy.html

Poison Oak and Poison Ivy Dermatitis: Prevention and Treat in Forest Service Work
by W.L. Epstein. and V.S. Byers
U.S. Dept. of Agriculture Forest Service, publication 8167 2803 (1981)

SECTION 9
PI Reader

Few plants have been so historically researched as poison oak and ivy — a chance to be intimate with danger, yet bear none of the rash risks. Its entire species, Toxicodendron, and family, Anacardiaceae, are endlessly fascinating.

Section 9 / Chapters 1 - 2
Strange Facts & Terrible Tales
Debunking the Bull Manure

Specialized sources of information: Anacardiaceae family

Anacardiaceae **(cashew family)**
https://en.wikipedia.org/wiki/Anacardiaceae

Cardanol
https://en.wikipedia.org/wiki/Cardanol

Cashew
https://en.wikipedia.org/wiki/Cashew

Cross-reactivity between papaya, mango and cashew
American Academy of Allergy, Asthma & Immunology
http://www.aaaai.org/ask-the-expert/cross-reactivity-papaya-mango-cashew.aspx

Ethnobotany of poison ivy, poison oak, and relatives (Toxicodendron spp., Anacardiaceae) in America: Veracity of historical accounts
by David S. Senchina
Rhodora October 2006 : Vol. 108, Issue 935 (Oct 2006), pg(s) 203-227

International Poisonous Plants Checklist: An Evidence-Based Reference
by D. Jesse Wagstaff
https://books.google.com/books?id=h7tbd-5ZAQ8C&printsec=frontcover#v=onepage&q&f=false

Mango
https://en.wikipedia.org/wiki/Mango

Metopium toxiferum **(poisonwood)**
https://en.wikipedia.org/wiki/Metopium_toxiferum

Pistachio
https://en.wikipedia.org/wiki/Pistachio

Phenolic Resins: Chemistry, Applications, Standardization, Safety and Ecology
by A. Gardziella, L.A. Pilato, A. Knop
https://books.google.com/books?id=NsvyCAAAQBAJ&printsec=frontcover&source=gbs_atb#v=onepage&q&f=false

Poison Ivy, Poison Oak, Poison Sumac and Their Relatives; Pistachios, Mangoes and Cashews
by Edward Frankel, Ph.D. 1991.
The Boxwood Press. Pacific Grove, Calif. ISBN 0-940168-18-9

The Poisoned Weed: Plants Toxic to Skin: Plants Toxic to Skin
By Donald G. Crosby, Professor Emeritus, Department of Environmental Toxicology University of California-Davis
https://books.google.com/books?id=W4D1H-1PEL-AC&pg=PA25&dq#v

Preparation and characterization of brake linings from modified tannin-phenol formaldehyde resin and asbestos-free fillers
http://link.springer.com/article/10.1007%2Fs10853-005-2396-7#page-1

Schinus terebinthifolius **(Brazilian peppertree)**
https://en.wikipedia.org/wiki/Schinus_terebinthifolius

Specialized sources of information: Toxicodendron species

The Generall Historie of Virginia, New-England, and the Summer Isles
by Captain John Smith
http://www.americanjourneys.org/pdf/AJ-082.pdf

Indian Herbalogy of North America
by Alma R. Hutchens
https://books.google.com/books?id=icuLw-pIkH2oC&printsec=frontcover&dq=#v=onepage&q&f=false

Japan wax
https://en.wikipedia.org/wiki/Japan_wax

Poison ivy (disambiguation)
https://en.wikipedia.org/wiki/Poison_ivy_%28disambiguation%29

Poison Oak Show
http://www.columbiacalifornia.com/scsaloon.html

Prospects and potential of fatty acid methyl esters of some non-traditional seed oils for use as biodiesel in India
Biomass and Bioenergy, Volume 29, Issue 4, October 2005, Pages 293–302
https://www.researchgate.net/publication/222394478_Azan_M_M_Waris_A_and_Nahar_N_M_Prospects_and_potential_of_fatty_acid_methyl_esters_of_some_non-traditional_seed_oils_for_use_as_biodiesel_in_India_Biomass_Bioenergy

Sokushinbutsu: The Bizarre Practice of Self Mummification | Amusing Planet
http://www.amusingplanet.com/2012/01/sokushinbutsu-bizarre-practice-of-self.html

Toxicodendron **(genus)**
https://en.wikipedia.org/wiki/Toxicodendron

Toxicodendron striatum **(manzanillo)**
https://en.wikipedia.org/wiki/Toxicodendron_striatum

Toxicodendron vernicifluum **(Japanese lacquer tree)**
http://en.wikipedia.org/wiki/Toxicodendron_vernicifluum

Toxicodendron succedaneum **(Japanese wax tree)**
https://en.wikipedia.org/wiki/Toxicodendron_succedaneum

Illustration and Photo Credits

Book design and production: Scooter Smith

Cover and section heads photo: Poison Ivy Vines
©Mark Kostich, istockphoto.com

Section 1 / Chapter 1

PI Ninja
©2016 Scooter Smith

Captain John Smith
STC 22790, Houghton Library, Harvard University. Alterations by Scooter Smith.

Section 3 / Chapter 1

Layers of the Skin
©2016 Scooter Smith

Allergic Contact Dermatitis
©2016 Scooter Smith

Section 1 / Chapter 1

PI Ninja
©2016 Scooter Smith

Section 4 / Chapter 3

PI Ninja
©2016 Scooter Smith

Section 4 / Chapter 4

Aloe Vera
"Aloe vera flower inset" by Collage by en:User:MidgleyDJ, original images from Wikimedia commons (Image:Aloe_vera_offsets.jpg and Image:Aloe_vera_C.jpg). Original uploader was MidgleyDJ at en.wikipedia - Transferred from en.wikipedia; transferred to Commons by User:Andrei Stroe using CommonsHelper.(Original text : See author.). Licensed under CC BY-SA 3.0 via Wikimedia Commons. Cropped by Scooter Smith.

Borage
"*Borago officinalis*, two blossoms" by Hans Bernhard (Schnobby) - Own work. Licensed under CC BY-SA 3.0 via Wikimedia Commons - http://commons.wikimedia.org/wiki/File:Borago_officinalis_two_blossoms.jpg#/media/File:Borago_officinalis_two_blossoms.jpg

Burdock
"*ArctiumLappa1*" by Christian Fischer. Licensed under CC BY-SA 3.0 via Wikimedia Commons - http://commons.wikimedia.org/wiki/File:ArctiumLappa1.jpg#/media/File:ArctiumLappa1.jpg

Calendula
"Flower July 2013-2" by Alvesgaspar - Own work. Licensed under CC BY-SA 3.0 via Wikimedia Commons - http://commons.wikimedia.org/wiki/File:Flower_July_2013-2.jpg#/media/File:Flower_July_2013-2.jpg

Camphor
"*Cinnamomum camphora* Turramurra railway" by Poyt448 Peter Woodard - Own work. Licensed under CC0 via Wikimedia Commons - http://commons.wikimedia.org/wiki/File:Cinnamomum_camphora_Turramurra_railway.jpg#/media/File:Cinnamomum_camphora_Turramurra_railway.jpg

Chamomile, German
"*Matricaria* February 2008-1" by Alvesgaspar - Own work. Licensed under CC BY-SA 3.0 via Wikimedia Commons - http://commons.wikimedia.org/wiki/File:Matricaria_February_2008-1.jpg#/media/File:Matricaria_February_2008-1.jpg

Cilantro
"Cilantro plants" by HitroMilanese - Own work. Licensed under CC BY-SA 3.0 via Wikimedia Commons - http://commons.wikimedia.org/wiki/File:Cilantro_plants.jpg#/media/File:Cilantro_plants.jpg

Coleus
"*Plectranthus barbatus*" by mauroguanandi - http://www.flickr.com/photos/mauroguanandi/3197358136/. Licensed under CC BY 2.0 via Wikimedia Commons - http://commons.wikimedia.org/wiki/File:Plectranthus_barbatus.jpg#/media/File:Plectranthus_barbatus.jpg

Comfrey
"*Symphytum officinale* 01" by Nova - Own work. Licensed under CC BY 2.5 via Wikimedia Commons - http://commons.wikimedia.org/wiki/File:Symphytum_officinale_01.jpg#/media/File:Symphytum_officinale_01.jpg

Echinacea
"Purple Coneflower (Echinacea purpurea)-1" by Jmeeter - Own work. Licensed under Public Domain via Wikimedia Commons - http://commons.wikimedia.org/wiki/File:Purple_Coneflower_(Echinacea_purpurea)-1.JPG#/media/File:Purple_Coneflower_(Echinacea_purpurea)-1.JPG

Eucalyptus, blue gum
"Starr 031002-0027 Eucalyptus globulus" by Forest & Kim Starr. Licensed under CC BY 3.0 via Wikimedia Commons - http://commons.wikimedia.org/wiki/File:Starr_031002-0027_Eucalyptus_globulus.jpg#/media/File:Starr_031002-0027_Eucalyptus_globulus.jpg. Cropped by Scooter Smith.

Evening Primrose
"Oenothera × fallax 001" by Georges Jansoone User:JoJan - Own work (own photo). Licensed under Public Domain via Wikimedia Commons - http://commons.wikimedia.org/wiki/File:Oenothera_%C3%97_fallax_001.jpg#/media/File:Oenothera_%C3%97_fallax_001.jpg

Goldenseal
"*Hydrastis*" by James Steakley - Own work. Licensed under CC BY-SA 3.0 via Wikimedia Commons - http://commons.wikimedia.org/wiki/File:Hydrastis.jpg#/media/File:Hydrastis.jpg

Grindelia
"*Grindelia robusta*". Licensed under CC BY-SA 3.0 via Wikimedia Commons - http://commons.wikimedia.org/wiki/File:Grindelia_robusta.jpg#/media/File:Grindelia_robusta.jpg

Helichrysum
"*Helichrysum italicum* flowers" by Júlio Reis - Own work. Licensed under CC BY-SA 3.0 via Wikimedia Commons - http://commons.wikimedia.org/wiki/File:Helichrysum_italicum_flowers.jpg#/media/File:Helichrysum_italicum_flowers.jpg

Horse Chestnut
"*Aesculus hippocastanum* fruit" by Solipsist - Own work. Licensed under CC BY-SA 2.0 via Wikimedia Commons - http://commons.wikimedia.org/wiki/File:Aesculus_hippocastanum_fruit.jpg#/media/File:Aesculus_hippocastanum_fruit.jpg

Jewelweed
"Potapsco fg13" by Fritz Geller-Grimm - Own work. Licensed under CC BY-SA 2.5 via Wikimedia Commons - http://commons.wikimedia.org/wiki/File:Potapsco_fg13.jpg#/media/File:Potapsco_fg13.jpg

Lavender, true
© Fotokon | Dreamstime.com - Lavender Plant Photo

Mint
"Minze" by Simon Eugster --Simon 13:07, 2 July 2006 (UTC) - Own work. Licensed under CC BY-SA 3.0 via Wikimedia Commons - http://commons.wikimedia.org/wiki/File:Minze.jpg#/media/File:Minze.jpg

Oats
"*Avena sativa* 002" by H. Zell - Own work. Licensed under CC BY 3.0 via Wikimedia Commons - http://commons.wikimedia.org/wiki/File:Avena_sativa_002.JPG#/media/File:Avena_sativa_002.JPG

Plantain
"Ribwort 600" by sannse - Originally uploaded to English Wikipedia as Ribwort 600.jpg. Licensed under CC BY-SA 3.0 via Wikimedia Commons - http://commons.wikimedia.org/wiki/File:Ribwort_600.jpg#/media/File:Ribwort_600.jpg

Rose hips
"Aubépines - Loire et Cher 02" by Dinkum - Own work. Licensed under CC0 via Wikimedia Commons - http://commons.wikimedia.org/wiki/File:Aub%C3%A9pines_-_Loire_et_Cher_02.JPG#/media/File:Aub%C3%A9pines_-_Loire_et_Cher_02.JPG

Rosemary
"*Rosmarinus officinalis*133095382" by THOR - Flowering Rosemary. Licensed under CC BY 2.0 via Wikimedia Commons - http://commons.wikimedia.org/wiki/File:Rosmarinus_officinalis133095382.jpg#/media/File:Rosmarinus_officinalis133095382.jpg

Sassafras
"Sassafras7" by Original uploader was Wowbobwow12 at en.wikipedia - Transferred from en.wikipedia; transferred to Commons using CommonsHelper.. Licensed under CC BY-SA 3.0 via Wikimedia Commons - http://commons.wikimedia.org/wiki/File:Sassafras7.jpg#/media/File:Sassafras7.jpg

Tea, black
"Çay-1" by Karduelis - Own work. Licensed under Public Domain via Wikimedia Commons - http://commons.wikimedia.org/wiki/File:%C3%87ay-1.jpg#/media/File:%C3%87ay-1.jpg

Tea tree
"*Melaleuca alternifolia* (Maria Serena)" by Tangopaso - Own work. Licensed under Public Domain via Wikimedia Commons - http://commons.wikimedia.org/wiki/File:Melaleuca_alternifolia_(Maria_Serena).jpg#/media/File:Melaleuca_alternifolia_(Maria_Serena).jpg

Turmeric
"*Curcuma longa* 001" by H. Zell - Own work. Licensed under CC BY-SA 3.0 via Wikimedia Commons - http://commons.wikimedia.org/wiki/File:Curcuma_longa_001.JPG#/media/File:Curcuma_longa_001.JPG

White oak
"White oak foliage". Licensed under Public Domain via Wikimedia Commons - http://commons.wikimedia.org/wiki/File:White_oak_foliage.JPG#/media/File:White_oak_foliage.JPG. Cropped by Scooter Smith.

Witch hazel
"*Hamamelis virginiana* FlowersLeaves BotGardBln0906". Licensed under CC BY-SA 3.0 via Wikimedia Commons - http://commons.wikimedia.org/wiki/File:Hamamelis_virginiana_FlowersLeaves_BotGardBln0906.JPG#/media/File:Hamamelis_virginiana_FlowersLeaves_BotGardBln0906.JPG

Essential oils bottle
"SandalwoodEssOil" by Itineranttrader - Own work. Licensed under Public Domain via Wikimedia Commons - http://commons.wikimedia.org/wiki/File:SandalwoodEssOil.png#/media/File:SandalwoodEssOil.png

Section 6 / Chapter 1

Red leaves on Eastern poison ivy
Toxicodendron radicans 002" by H. Zell - Own work. Licensed under CC BY-SA 3.0 via Wikimedia Commons - http://commons.wikimedia.org/wiki/File:Toxicodendron_radicans_002.JPG#/media/File:Toxicodendron_radicans_002.JPG

Eastern poison ivy - summer
©2016 Scooter Smith

Eastern poison ivy stems - winter
©2016 Scooter Smith

Eastern poison ivy vines climbing tree - summer
©2016 Scooter Smith

Eastern poison ivy berries - summer
©2016 Scooter Smith

Range of Eastern poison ivy map
©2016 Scooter Smith; resources: Biota of North America Program's North American Plant Atlas - bonap.net; Encyclopedia of Life - EOL.org; poison-ivy.org; Mountain High Maps™ ©1994 Digital Wisdom Inc.

Eastern poison ivy first leaf - early spring
©2016 Scooter Smith

Eastern poison ivy berries - winter
©2016 Scooter Smith

Eastern poison ivy bush
©2016 Scooter Smith

Eastern poison ivy vines and dead leaves - late fall
©2016 Scooter Smith

Western poison oak leaf
tora2_002_php.jpg - Jennifer Anderson, hosted by the USDA-NRCS PLANTS Database

Western poison oak with flowers
"*Toxicodendron diversilobum* 1" by Franz Xaver - Own work. Licensed under CC BY-SA 3.0 via Wikimedia Commons - http://commons.wikimedia.org/wiki/File:Toxicodendron_diversilobum_1.jpg#/media/File:Toxicodendron_diversilobum_1.jpg

Western poison oak berries - late fall
"*Toxicodendron diversilobum* berries" by Noah Elhardt - Own work. Licensed under CC BY-SA 2.5 via Wikimedia Commons - http://commons.wikimedia.org/wiki/File:Toxicodendron_diversilobum_berries.jpg#/media/File:Toxicodendron_diversilobum_berries.jpg

Range of Western poison oak map
©2016 Scooter Smith; resources: Biota of North America Program's North American Plant Atlas - bonap.net; Encyclopedia of Life - EOL.org; poison-ivy.org; Mountain High Maps™ ©1994 Digital Wisdom Inc.

Western poison oak bush - fall
"Toxicodendron diversilobum (poison oak) -- Topanga Canyon, Los Angeles County" by Joe Decruyenaere - own work. Licensed under CC BY-SA 2.0 via Wikimedia Commons - https://commons.wikimedia.org/wiki/File:Toxicodendron_diversilobum_001.jpg#/media/File:Toxicodendron_diversilobum_001.jpg

Eastern poison oak
topu2_006_pvp.jpg - jeffm@almostedenplants.com - Jeff McMillian, hosted by the USDA-NRCS PLANTS Database

Eastern poison oak leaves
toqu_001_php.jpg - Robert H. Mohlenbrock, hosted by the USDA-NRCS PLANTS Database / USDA SCS. 1991. Southern wetland flora: Field office guide to plant species. South National Technical Center, Fort Worth.

Eastern poison oak flowers
topu2_004_pvp.jpg - Jeff McMillian, hosted by the USDA-NRCS PLANTS Database

Range of Eastern poison oak map
©2016 Scooter Smith; resources: Biota of North America Program's North American Plant Atlas - bonap.net; Encyclopedia of Life - EOL.org; poison-ivy.org; Mountain High Maps™ ©1994 Digital Wisdom Inc.

Eastern poison oak berries
topu2_007_pvp.jpg - Jeff McMillian, hosted by the USDA-NRCS PLANTS Database

Rydberg's poison ivy
Toxicodendron rydbergii UGA1208036" by Dave Powell, USDA Forest Service, Bugwood.org (cropped by the uploader) - Forestry Images, Image Number: 1208036. Licensed under CC BY 3.0 via Wikimedia Commons - http://commons.wikimedia.org/wiki/File:Toxicodendron_rydbergii_UGA1208036.jpg#/media/File:Toxicodendron_rydbergii_UGA1208036.jpg

Rydberg's poison ivy flowers
"*Toxicodendron rydbergii* NPS-1" by Lee Ferguson - http://www.nps.gov/archive/arch/flowers/Yellow_flowers/Anacardiaceae_Toxicodendron_rydbergii2.htm. Licensed under Public Domain via Wikimedia Commons - http://commons.wikimedia.org/wiki/File:Toxicodendron_rydbergii_NPS-1.jpg#/media/File:Toxicodendron_rydbergii_NPS-1.jpg

Range of Rydberg's poison ivy map
©2016 Scooter Smith; resources: Biota of North America Program's North American Plant Atlas - bonap.net; Encyclopedia of Life - EOL.org; poison-ivy.org; Mountain High Maps™ ©1994 Digital Wisdom Inc.

Rydberg's poison ivy berries
"*Toxicodendron rydbergii* UGA5369905" by Whitney Cranshaw, Colorado State University, United States, Bugwood.org - Forestry Images, Image Number: 5369905. Licensed under CC BY 3.0 via Wikimedia Commons - http://commons.wikimedia.org/wiki/File:Toxicodendron_rydbergii_UGA5369905.jpg#/media/File:Toxicodendron_rydbergii_UGA5369905.jpg

Rydberg's poison ivy - young
"Toxicodendron rydbergii UGA1208035" by Dave Powell, USDA Forest Service, Bugwood.org (cropped by the uploader) - Forestry Images, Image Number: 1208035. Licensed under CC BY 3.0 via Wikimedia Commons - http://commons.wikimedia.org/wiki/File:Toxicodendron_rydbergii_UGA1208035.jpg#/media/File:Toxicodendron_rydbergii_UGA1208035.jpg

Poison sumac bush
tove_003_php.jpg - norman_melvin@usgs.gov - Norman Melvin, hosted by the USDA-NRCS PLANTS Database

Poison sumac flowers
tove_008_pvp.jpg - jeffm@almostedenplants.com - Jeff McMillian, hosted by the USDA-NRCS PLANTS Database

Range of poison sumac map
©2015 Scooter Smith; resources: Biota of North America Program's North American Plant Atlas - bonap.net; Encyclopedia of Life - EOL.org; poison-ivy.org; Mountain High Maps™ ©1994 Digital Wisdom Inc.

Poison sumac leaf - fall
tove_002_php.jpg - Robert H. Mohlenbrock, hosted by the USDA-NRCS PLANTS Database / USDA SCS. 1991. Southern wetland flora: Field office guide to plant species. South National Technical Center, Fort Worth.

Section 6 / Chapter 2

Trifoliate leaf
©2016 Scooter Smith

Ground vine
©2016 Scooter Smith

Rhizomes
©2016 Scooter Smith

Eastern poison ivy berries
©2016 Scooter Smith

Virginia creeper
"Jonathan h4". Licensed under Public Domain via Wikimedia Commons - http://commons.wikimedia.org/wiki/File:Jonathan_h4.jpg#/media/File:Jonathan_h4.jpg

Box elder
"Acer negundo californicum Tehachapi" by Joe Decruyenaere - DSCN3959. Licensed under CC BY-SA 2.0 via Wikimedia Commons - http://commons.wikimedia.org/wiki/File:Acer_negundo_californicum_Tehachapi.jpg#/media/File:Acer_negundo_californicum_Tehachapi.jpg

Aromatic sumac
"Rhus aromatica NPS-1" by Jim Pisarowicz - http://www.nps.gov/wica/photosmultimedia/photo%2Dgallery%2Dtrees%2Dand%2Dshrubs%2E-htm?eid=133313&aId=172&root_aid=172&sort=title&startRow=46#e_133313. Licensed under Public Domain via Wikimedia Commons - http://commons.wikimedia.org/wiki/File:Rhus_aromatica_NPS-1.jpg#/media/File:Rhus_aromatica_NPS-1.jpg

Blackberry
"Starr 051123-5457 *Rubus* discolor" by Forest & Kim Starr. Licensed under CC BY 3.0 via Wikimedia Commons - http://commons.wikimedia.org/wiki/File:Starr_051123-5457_Rubus_discolor.jpg#/media/File:Starr_051123-5457_Rubus_discolor.jpg

Bladdernut
By R. A. Nonenmacher (Own work) [CC BY-SA 4.0 (http://creativecommons.org/licenses/by-sa/4.0)], via Wikimedia Commons - http://commons.wikimedia.org/wiki/File%3AStaphylea_trifolia_SCA-5111.jpg

Boston ivy
"WilderWein" by IKAl - Own work. Licensed under CC BY-SA 2.5 via Wikimedia Commons - http://commons.wikimedia.org/wiki/File:WilderWein.jpg#/media/File:WilderWein.jpg

Hop tree
Ptelea trifoliata 20050606 644 2". Licensed under CC BY-SA 3.0 via Wikimedia Commons - http://commons.wikimedia.org/wiki/File:Ptelea_trifoliata_20050606_644_2.jpg#/media/File:Ptelea_trifoliata_20050606_644_2.jpg

Jack in the pulpit
"Arisaema triphyllum plant" by Daniel Schwen - Own work. Licensed under CC BY-SA 4.0 via Wikime-

dia Commons - http://commons.wikimedia.org/wiki/File:Arisaema_triphyllum_plant.jpg#/media/File:Arisaema_triphyllum_plant.jpg

Sassafras
"Sassafras7" by Original uploader was Wowbobwow12 at en.wikipedia - Transferred from en.wikipedia; transferred to Commons using CommonsHelper.. Licensed under CC BY-SA 3.0 via Wikimedia Commons - http://commons.wikimedia.org/wiki/File:Sassafras7.jpg#/media/File:Sassafras7.jpg

Section 8 / Chapter 2

Fiskars PowerGear® lopper
  photo by Scooter Smith

Fiskars PowerStik® lopper
  photo by Scooter Smith

Resources

Amy Martin
  photo by Marla McDonald

About the Author

Over her varied journalism career of more than four decades, Amy Martin has covered petroleum science and environmental issues, written trail reviews of parks and preserves, penned a book on herbology, and even served as a comedy critic. She operated a North Texas news service for 15 years specializing in holistic health and other alternative topics. During their 12 years of managing a private nature preserve, Martin and her husband Scooter Smith engaged in regular battle with poison ivy. All these come together in Itchy Business.

Martin is known for articulating complex, provocative and sometimes highly technical issues in a coherent and comprehensive way, but also eloquent and lightheartedly wry. She has been employed by the Dallas Morning News (recycling), Dallas Observer (music), and Dallas Times Herald (performing arts and features), and freelanced for many others. She was contributing editor and columnist for the national magazine Garbage (recycling and features). Martin is currently senior comedy critic for the Dallas performing arts website TheaterJones, North Texas Wild columnist for GreenSource DFW, and The Aging Hippie columnist for Senior Voice. Her personal website is www.Moonlady.com.

Made in the USA
San Bernardino, CA
07 April 2016